2D AutoCAD for Students

Alf Yarwood

Hodder & Stoughton
LONDON SYDNEY AUCKLAND

Orders: please contact Bookpoint Ltd, 130 Milton Park, Abingdon, Oxon OX14 4SB. Telephone: (44) 01235 827720. Fax: (44) 01235 400454. Lines are open from 9.00 - 6.00, Monday to Saturday, with a 24 hour message answering service. You can also order through our website www.hodderheadline.co.uk.

British Library Cataloguing in Publication Data
A catalogue record for this title is available from the British Library

ISBN 0 340 873043

First Published 2003
Impression number   10 9 8 7 6 5 4 3 2 1
Year   2007   2006   2005   2004   2003

Cover image from Alfred Pasieka/Science Photo Library
Typeset by Phoenix Photosetting, Chatham, Kent
Printed in Great Britain for Hodder & Stoughton Educational, a division of Hodder Headline Plc, 338 Euston Road, London NW1 3BH by Arrowsmiths Ltd

ii

Contents

iii

Preface

This book is designed to be used as course work for those wishing to learn how to construct two-dimensional drawings (2D) using the computer-aided design software package **AutoCAD®**. Although all the illustrations have been taken from, or constructed in, AutoCAD 2004, the book's contents are just as suitable for those who are using earlier **Windows®** releases of the software. There have been some additions to AutoCAD 2004 over earlier releases, but these do not affect the use of this book.

Two-dimensional drawing is still the most widely used method of constructing technical drawings in industry despite the increasing use of three-dimensional (3D) drawings. Because of this, the book's contents are suitable for all those who wish to undertake courses involving learning how to use AutoCAD software – beginners taking courses involving CAD, those working at home, students at colleges of Further Education and operators working in industry. The book is particularly suited for students taking courses aimed at City and Guilds 4353 2D Computer Aided Design Level 2 and 3.

The book's pages contain a number of graded examples, worked examples and assignments suitable for those beginning to learn how to use the software. Its contents are intended for use by those who have not had any experience using AutoCAD and are coming new to the software. It is, however, assumed the reader has an elementary knowledge of working with a computer and in particular with Windows as the operating system under which the computer is functioning. The idea behind the book is that, sitting in front of a computer with AutoCAD loaded and with the book opened at an appropriate page and by closely following the instructions given for the examples and worked examples, the reader will, by the end of each chapter, be able to construct drawings as answers to the assignments.

AutoCAD is a very complex software system. A book the size of this cannot possibly cover the complexities of all the methods of construction available when operating the software. It is however hoped that, by the time the reader has worked through the contents of this book, he/she will have gained sufficient skill and knowledge to be able to go on to more advanced constructions and have gained an interest in the more advanced possibilities available when using AutoCAD for the construction of 2D technical drawings.

Alf Yarwood   Salisbury 2003

Acknowledgements

Registered Trademarks

The following are registered in the US Patent and Trademark Office by Autodesk Inc.:

Autodesk®, AutoCAD®.

Windows® is a registered trademark of the Microsoft Corporation.

Alf Yarwood is a member of the Autodesk Advanced Developer Network and a Master Developer with Autodesk Ltd.

Chapter One

The Principles of 2D CAD

Loading AutoCAD

When a computer running under Windows is switched on, after the software files have loaded, the Windows desktop appears. To load AutoCAD:

1. *Double-click* on the **AutoCAD** short-cut icon or.

2. *Right-click* on the **AutoCAD** short-cut icon, followed by a *left-click* on **Open** in the menu which appears on the screen.

Whichever method is used, the **AutoCAD** window appears on the screen.

The names of the parts of the AutoCAD window are shown in the illustration below. Usually there are normally five toolbars showing in the window:

■ The **Standard** toolbar at the top of the window.

■ The **Styles** toolbar *docked* to the right of the **Standard** toolbar.

■ The **Layers** toolbar *docked* below the **Standard** toolbar

■ The **Draw** toolbar *docked* at the left-hand side of the AutoCAD window.

■ The **Modify** toolbar *docked* on the right of the **Draw** toolbar.

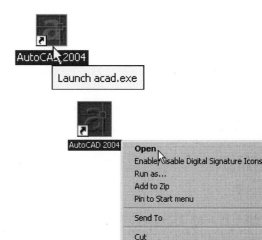

Most of the AutoCAD window is taken up by the drawing area, within which drawings can be constructed.

1. Minimise, Maximise and Close buttons to both the AutoCAD window and to the drawing area of the window.

2. *Left-click* on the AutoCAD Minimise button and the window closes, but appears in the Windows task bar as an icon.

Notes

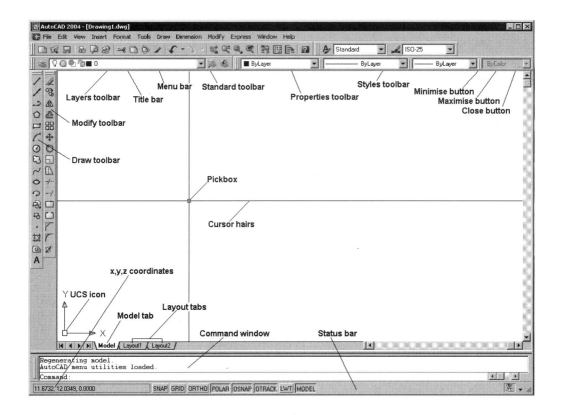

Terms used throughout this book

Left-click – Place the cursor under mouse control onto a feature and press the *pick* button of the mouse. Shown in this book in italics – *left-click*.

Right-click – Press the *Return* button of the mouse. Shown in this book in italics – *right-click*. The same result can be achieved by pressing the **Enter** or *Return* key of the keyboard.

Double-click – Place the cursor under mouse control onto a feature and press the *pick* button of the mouse twice in rapid succession. Shown in this book in italics – *double-click*.

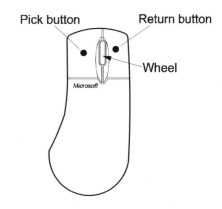

Drag – Move the cursor under mouse control, hold down the *pick* button and move the mouse. The feature moves with the mouse movement. Shown in this book in italics – *drag*.

Select – Move the cursor onto a feature and press the *pick* button of the mouse.

Pick – A similar action as select. The two terms are used throughout this book and can be regarded as having the same meaning. Shown in this book in italics – *pick*.

Pick button – the left hand button of the mouse.

Pick box – An adjustable square associated with picking features of a construction.

Enter – Type the given word or letters at the keyboard. Shown in this book in italics – *enter*.

Return – Press the **Return** or **Enter** key of the keyboard. Usually, but not always, has the same result as a *right-click*. Shown in this book in italics – *Return*.

Esc – The **Esc** key of the keyboard. In AutoCAD pressing the **Esc** key has the effect of cancelling the current action taking place.

Tab key – The key usually on the left hand side of the keyboard which carries two arrows.

Tool – The same as a command in earlier releases of AutoCAD.

Icons – A common graphic feature in all Windows applications – a small item of graphics representing a tool or a function of the software in use.

Flyout – A number of tool icons have a small arrow in the bottom right-hand corner of the icon. Such icons will produce a flyout when the cursor is placed onto the icon and the *pick* button of the mouse is held down.

Default – The name given to the settings or parameters of an application as set when the software is first purchased.

Objects – Individual lines, circles etc. as drawn in AutoCAD. When objects are grouped together as groups or as blocks the whole group will be treated as an object.

Entity – Has the same meaning in AutoCAD, as has the word object.

Tool tip – The name of the tool represented by an icon, which appears when the cursor under mouse control is placed onto a tool icon.

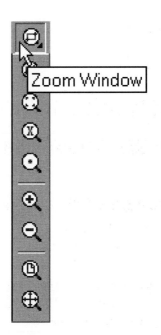

Toolbars

When first loaded the AutoCAD window includes five toolbars. Other toolbars can be called by:

- *Right-click* in any part of a toolbar on screen. The **Toolbars** list appears.

- *Left-click* in the list against the name of the required toolbar. The selected toolbar appears.

Toolbars can be either *docked* against either side, at the top or at the bottom of the AutoCAD window. *Docked* toolbars can be *dragged* on screen using the *drag* bars at the top of the *docked* toolbars. They can be resized while on screen by *dragging* at the edges of the toolbar. When not *docked* toolbars are said to be *floating*.

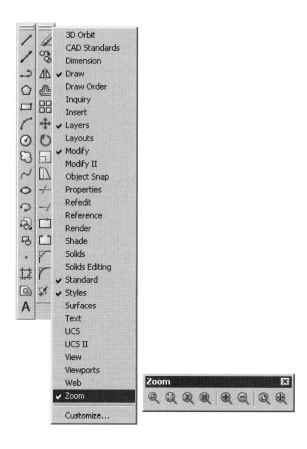

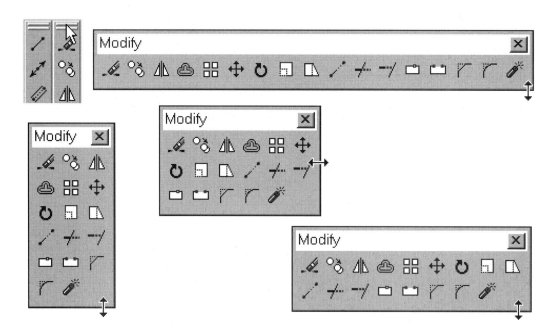

Dialogs

Several types of boxes will be seen when operating AutoCAD – dialogs, messages and warnings. The most important of these are the numerous dialogs. These vary in appearance and the way in which they are laid out, but have common features, some of which are shown below.

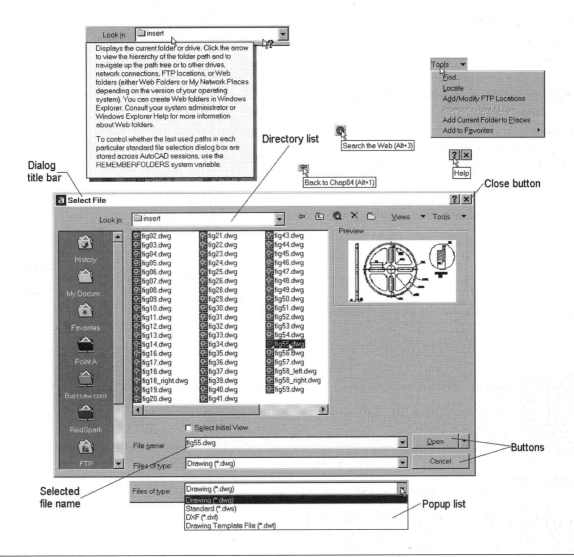

Notes

1. A popup list will appear, with a *left-click* on a downward pointing arrow positioned on the right of a window within a dialogue box.

2. If a question mark (**?**) within a small button is positioned at the top right of a dialogue box, a *left-click* on the button, followed by another on any part of the dialogue box, brings up a help box showing the function of that part of the dialogue box.

The AutoCAD Help system

There are three main methods of calling for help in AutoCAD.

Method 1

Left-click on **Help** in the menu bar and again on **Help** in the drop-down menu which appears. A dialog **AutoCAD. Help: User Documentation** appears. *Enter* the words of the topic you are seeking, then *left-click* on the **List Topics** button. Select an item from the list which appears. The Help details for that topic appear in the dialog.

Method 2

Left-click on **Help** in the menu bar and on **Active Assistance** in the drop-down menu which appears. When a tool is called, **Help** details automatically appear in the **Active Assistance** dialog, which will be on screen.

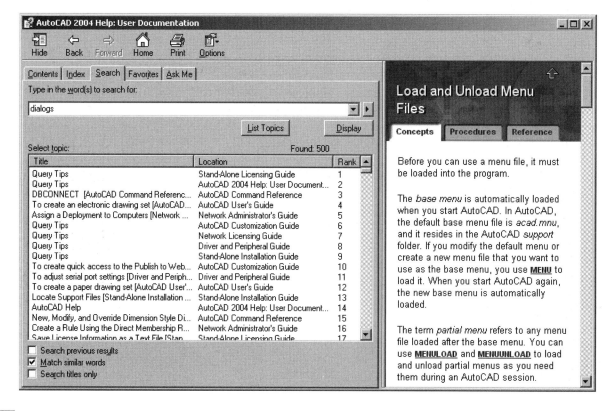

Method 3

When using any tool, press the **F1** key and the **Help** window for the tool in use appears. This form of help is known as associative – it is associated with the tool in action.

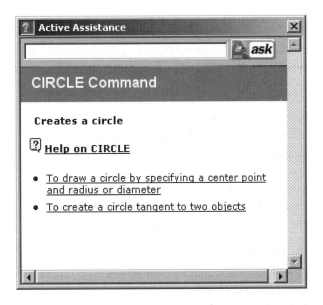

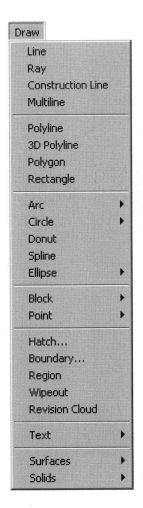

AutoCAD menus

There are several types of menus available when using AutoCAD, including:

Drop-down menus: A *left-click* on a name in the menu bar of the AutoCAD window brings a **drop-down** menu on screen. As an example the **Draw** drop-down menu is shown. A *left-click* on the name of a tool in this menu makes that tool operative.

Right-click menus: As an example, a *right-click* in the **Layout1** tab brings a right-click menu on screen, from which choices may be made.

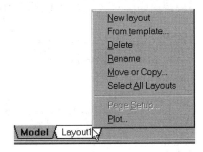

Directories and files

To see the drives, directories and files held on a
computer, *right-click* on the short-cut icon labelled
Windows Explorer in the Windows desktop,
followed by a *left-click* on **Open** in the menu
which appears, or *double-click* on the short-cut
icon. The **Explorer** window appears.

In the **Explorer** window, directories and sub-
directories are shown as icons, some with a + icon
to the left of the directory icon. A *left-click* on the
+ icon opens the directory to show its contents and
the + icon changes to a - icon. When opened a
directory icon changes to appears like an opened
folder and the contents of the directory are shown
in the **Name** list of the **Explorer** window.

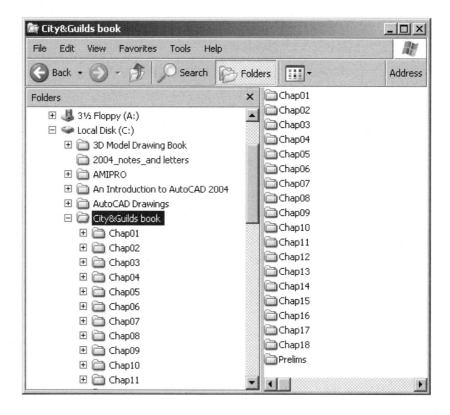

Everything that appears on a computer screen is either held, or can be saved as electronic data **files**. The majority of files are grouped into **directories** or sub-directories. The directories, sub-directories and files are held on disks fitted in the computer. In general there are three types of disk:

■ **Floppy disks** are removable and named **3½ inch Floppy (A:)**.

■ **Hard disks** are usually fixed and named as **C:**. More than one hard disk may be contained in a computer.

■ **CD-ROM disks** are removable and named as **D:**. More than one CD-ROM drive may be contained in a computer.

There are other types of disks in which a file can be saved – see page 12.

To Open, Print, Copy, Delete or Rename files

Files can be **opened**, **copied**, **deleted** or **renamed** while in the **Explorer** window. A *right-click* on a file name brings up a menu. In the menu a *left-click* on **Open**, opens the file, a *left-click* on **Print** and the file prints, a *left-click* on **Delete** brings up a warning box asking if the file should be sent to the **Recycle Bin**, a *left-click* on **Rename** highlights the file name and a new name can be *entered* over the old name.

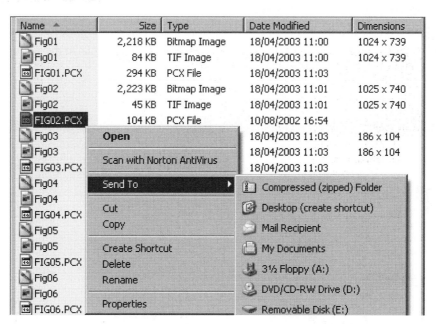

File name extensions

All files are given file name extensions depending upon the software application that was used to construct the file. Some examples are ***.dwg** (AutoCAD drawing files); **.txt** (text files); **.bmp** (bitmap files formed by using an application such as **Windows Paint**; **.sys** (system files for operating applications); **.doc** (**Windows Write** files). There are many more depending upon the application in use.

Backup files

When an AutoCAD drawing is constructed and saved to disk and further details added to the drawing, after which a second save is made, the first saved file becomes a **backup** file with a file extension name of **.bak**. As an example, if an AutoCAD drawing is saved as say, **extractor.dwg**, then when a second save is made with the same file name, the first saved file becomes **extractor.bak**. This system of forming backup files is not exclusive to AutoCAD. Other applications use the same precaution.

It is possible to rename an AutoCAD ***.bak** file as a ***.dwg** file by a *right-click* on its name in the **Explorer** window, which brings up the right-click menu shown on page 9. *Left-click* on **Rename** in the menu. The name of the ***.bak** file highlights. *Enter* on the highlighted file name a new name ending in ***.dwg** and the ***.bak** file becomes the AutoCAD drawing file which was originally backed-up.

Quite apart from these ***.bak** files, it is always advisable to save any drawings you may construct either to another disk or to another name. In this manner if something happens such as a computer crash when you are constructing a drawing, another copy of the drawing will be available. Personally, I save all drawings first to my **C:** hard disk and then also to an **A:** floppy disk.

The Program Files directory

One important directory containing a number of sub-directories is the **Program Files** directory. As shown below it contains the various software applications (including **AutoCAD**) in its contents.

The contents of the AutoCAD directory

Left-click on the + icon against the **Progam Files** directory name and again on the + icon against the **AutoCAD** directory name. Note the large number of directories and files held in the **AutoCAD** directory. Part of the directory contents are shown below.

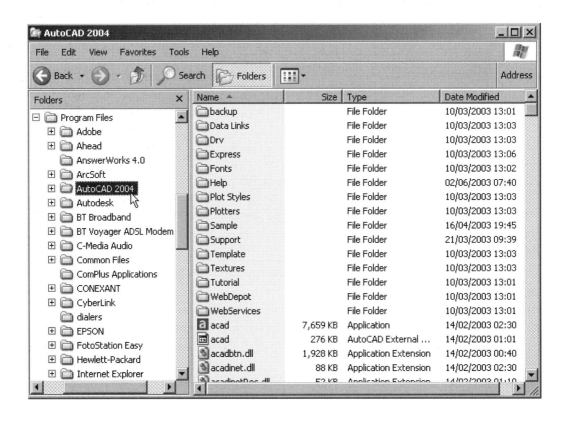

Computers

Computers vary considerably as to shape, speed of operation and the *peripherals* attached to them. Computers are the machinery (hardware) into which software applications such as AutoCAD can be loaded in order to perform operations such as (with AutoCAD) construct, save and print drawings. Many other software applications can be loaded into a computer to perform other tasks – such as word processors which can be use to produce typed documents.

Bits and bytes

The basis of operation of computers is in binary mathematics, which involves two digits 0 and 1. Each digit is a **bit** (short for binary digit). Bits are grouped into sequences of 8 forming a **byte**. 1024 bytes form a **Kilobyte (KB)**. 1024 KB form a **Megabyte (MG)** and 1024 Megabytes form a **Gigabyte (GB)**.

Coprocessors

Computers are run by coprocessors with speeds measured in **Hertz**. Each Hertz is 1 cycle per second. A **Megahertz (MHz)** is 1,000,000 Hertz. A **Gigahertz (GHz)** is 1000 MHz.

One of the most commonly used coprocessors is the **Pentium** manufactured by Intel. The Pentium 2 has speeds of operation of up to 300 MHz per second. The Pentium 3 has speeds up to 800 MHz per second and the Pentium 4 has speeds up to 3.2 GHz per second.

This means a computer equipped with a Pentium 4 coprocessor runs at up to 3.2 billion cycles per second (its **clock** speed). Each computer instruction requires a number of cycles (Hertz). This means that the clock speed controls the number of instructions per second a computer can perform.

AutoCAD 2004 is designed to operate with a minimum of a Pentium 3 coprocessor.

Operating systems

Computers are run under operating systems, which are themselves software applications loaded into the computer and designed to ensure that other software applications such as AutoCAD function as intended. The most common operating system in the world for PCs (personal computers) is Windows. There are several versions of Windows – Windows 3.1, Windows 95, Windows 98, Windows 2000, Windows NT and Windows XP, which have been added to and improved since Windows was first introduced. Windows is a multi-tasking operating system, which means that several software applications can be running at the same time – for example AutoCAD can be running at the same time as a word processor such as Microsoft Word and a graphic software such as Windows Paint and an operator can switch from one application to another without having to close down any one. The illustration shows AutoCAD opened at the same time as Windows Paint and Microsoft Word. By *clicking* on the application name in the Windows task bar, any one of the programmes can be opened.

Monitor screens (VDUs)

Monitor screens are also referred to as VDUs (Visual Display Units).

The images produced by operating software appear on a monitor screen. Monitors attached to PCs are usually one of two types – either a flat screen monitor, usually an LCD (Liquid Crystal Display) or a standard monitor. No matter which type of monitor is in use, what is seen on the monitor screen appears in sets of tiny coloured rectangular dots known as **pixels**.

The more pixels used to reproduce what is shown on a computer screen, the clearer will be the image that is displayed. Each pixel usually consists of three bytes (8-bit binary numbers). Three bytes in binary mathematics represents the values from 0 to 255.

Usually monitor screens are run by a system known as VGA (Video Graphics Array). The original VGA produced screens with 800x600 pixels. Later VGA screens can now have 1024x768, 1600x1200 or higher values. AutoCAD 2004 is designed to run in a screen of at least 1024x768.

Disks

A number of different types of disk are used in conjunction with computers in order to store directories, sub-directories and files to load into a computer or to be saved from what is created on a computer.

The following briefly describes the most commonly used disk types.

- **Hard disk** – all computers have at least one hard disk. This is a non-removable disk fitted permanently to the computer and on which software application files are held and on which practically all the work carried out on the computer is stored. Hard disks can carry large amounts of information.

- **Floppy disk** – a rectangular disk of a width of 3.5 inches, which can be fitted into a slot in the computer. The maximum amount of storage space on a 3.5 inch floppy is 1.4 MB. The disks are useful because they can be removed as necessary and easily carried from place to place. However their limitation is the small storage area of the disk.

- **CD** (Compact Disk) – a circular disk containing up to 750 MB of storage. Two types in common use are **CD-RW** (Compact Disk-Read Write), which can be written to for storing directories and files of work in progress and **CD ROM**, which is a read only disk that cannot be written to. Fits into a slot in the computer body and can be removed.

- **ZIP disks** – removable disks of three main storage types: 100 MB, 250 MB or 750 MB. Slotted in a computer which is fitted with a readable ZIP system, or slotted in an external ZIP driver.

Peripherals

A number of peripherals can be plugged via cables into a PC. PCs usually have a number of sockets (ports) into which cables connecting peripherals can be plugged. The most common sockets are **parallel** ports into which printers and plotters can be connected; **serial** ports into which a mouse can be connected and **USB** (Universal Serial Bus) ports which allow keyboards, mice, scanners, printers, modems and many other devices to be connected to a computer.

The most frequently used peripheral devices are:

■ **Monitor screen (VDU)** – on which images are constructed.

■ **Keyboard** – with the mouse, a keyboard is the major control device of a computer system.

■ **Mouse** – for controlling the position on screen of anything that is being constructed.

■ **Printers** – either black and white or coloured, for printing what is on the monitor screen on paper.

■ **Plotters** – mainly for printing drawings, such as when AutoCAD has been used to produce a drawing on screen.

■ **Scanners** – for copying documents, including drawings and photos to either a printer or to the monitor screen.

■ **External modem** – such as a Broadband modem for connecting to a telephone line.

■ **External drives** – such as for drives for ZIP disks, external CD drives, external hard disks.

Safety when using computers

There need be no serious risks to health when using computers. However problems can arise through such practises as:

■ adopting a poor seating position;

■ working in a bad work space;

■ poor lighting;

■ improper use of computer equipment;

■ not taking breaks from long working periods at a computer station.

Seating position

Before commencing work, adjust chair and VDU to what is considered to be the most comfortable position, with arms almost horizontal and eyes level with the VDU. Adjust the mouse and keyboard positions to their most comfortable positions. Move the VDU to a good viewing position. Make sure there is sufficient leg space for comfortable seating. A good working seat position should be with the back upright and the seat tilted slightly forward so as to avoid pressure on the back of the legs or knees.

Work space

There should be enough space around the computer for documents and other equipment. Document holders can save back and eye strain.

Lighting

Lighting of the work space should be glare free. Bright reflection of lights on the VDU screen can be tiring by causing eye strain. Lighting from natural sources or from artificial light should not be excessive.

Using the equipment

The keyboard is best positioned with desk space in front for placing the hands when not in use. Try to adopt a good keyboard technique.

Do not grip the mouse tightly when it is in use. Try to relax pressure on the mouse buttons.

The VDU screen needs to be clean and its brightness adjusted to suit your own requirements.

Do not detach or attach peripherals from the computer while it is running. It is always best to switch off the computer before doing so.

Take breaks from working

Never work at a computer station for long periods of time without rest. Take frequent short breaks from the work rather than single long breaks. Move the seating position occasionally. Take time off work at the computer by adopting other activities such as sorting documents, photocopying etc.

RSI (repetitive strain injury)

RSI includes aches and pains in the arms and shoulders, eye strain, headaches and stress. RSI can be considerably reduced, if not eliminated by following the guidelines already given above.

Eating and drinking

It is not advisable to eat or drink at a computer work station.

The World Wide Web

The World Wide Web (www) provides a valuable source of information. In order to be able to access this information, a computer must be equipped with a **modem** – either one fitted as a **card** inside the computer or fitted as an external peripheral. A modem is connected to a telephone line and it is through the telephone line that, via a modem, the computer can connect to the Internet.

Pages from the web may be in the form of text, pictures or sounds (such as background music). In order to bring web pages to a computer VDU, it is necessary to locate the address of the pages you require to view. Such an address is an URL (Uniform Resource Locator), which takes the form **www.autodesk.com**.

To assess the Web, *double-click* on the **Internet Explorer** start-up icon in the Windows desktop. The **MSN** search page appears. In the **Search** field enter **www.autodesk.com** and from the names in the area below the search field *left-click* on **Autodesk**. The web page which appears gives information about Autodesk products, Autodesk being the firm which publishes AutoCAD. A *left-click* in other parts of the page bring other information regarding Autodesk products on to screen.

Other items of information on any topic wished to be researched can be found by typing the name of the product, information or news which is required in the Search field.

The methods of searching for web pages vary between different forms of assessing the web, but the illustration given is typical of any other search method.

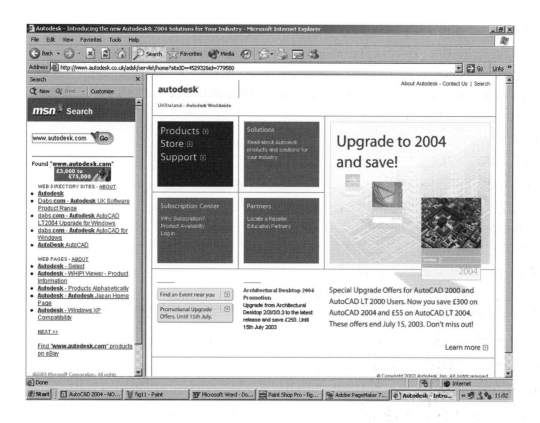

Simple drawing with AutoCAD

A drawing template

1. Open AutoCAD – *double-click* on its start-up icon in the Windows desktop.

2. In the command window at the bottom of the AutoCAD window *enter* **z** (abbreviation for **zoom**), followed by *entering* **a** (abbreviation for **All**).

```
Command: z
Specify corner of window, enter a scale factor (nX or nXP), or
[All/Center/Dynamic/Extents/Previous/Scale/Window] <real time>: a
Regenerating model.
Command:
```

3. In the command window *enter* **grid**, followed by *entering* **10**.

```
Command: grid
Specify grid spacing(X) or [ON/OFF/Snap/Aspect] <0.0000>: 10
Command:
```

4. In the command window *enter* **snap**, followed by *entering* **5**.

5. Move the mouse and note the changes in the coordinate unit numbers at the left-hand end of the status bar.

```
160.0000, 150.0000, 0.0000
```

The AutoCAD coordinate units system

Drawings are constructed in AutoCAD in either a 2D system or in a 3D system. When working in 2D the coordinates are expressed in terms of X and Y. X units are measured horizontally and Y units vertically. With this system, any point in the AutoCAD window can be referred to in terms of x,y. Thus the point $x,y = 40,50$ is 40 units horizontally to the right of an origin where $x,y = 0,0$ and 50 units vertically above the $x,y = 0,0$ origin. A number of 2D coordinate points in an AutoCAD 2004 window are shown.

The four decimal points after the coordinate numbers shown in the last illustration have been ignored for the purposes of this illustration. In this book we will be working mainly in coordinates with **0** decimal points.

Notes

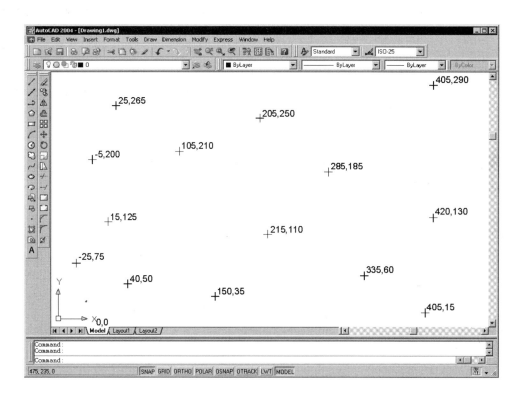

Coordinate points can be measured in negative figures. Thus the point $x,y = -100,-50$ is a point 100 units to the left of an origin $x,y = 0,0$ and 50 units below the origin $x,y = 0,0$.

3D coordinates include a third direction measured in terms of Z. In AutoCAD, +ve Z is as if coming towards the operator from the AutoCAD window perpendicular to the screen. This means that -ve Z is perpendicularly from the screen away from the operator. However this book is concerned only with 2D drawing so the Z coordinate number will be ignored.

Note that the coordinate reading in the prompt line of AutoCAD shows a three number coordinate e.g. *x,y,z* = 50,190,0. This is because when taking 2D coordinates Z units are at 0, that is, lying on the surface of the screen.

Grid and Snap

With **Grid** set to **10** a series of dots at regular spacings of 10 units in both the X and Y directions of the drawing area will be seen. Also showing will be the cross-hair cursor lines, the intersection of which move in response to movements of the mouse. Because **Snap** has been set to **5** as the mouse is moved so the cursor hairs jump in 5 unit jumps – they snap from one 5 unit point to another. **Grid** can be set on or off (toggled) by pressing the **F7** key and **Snap** can be toggled on/off by pressing the **F9** key. **Or** the buttons **SNAP** and **GRID** in the status bar can be set on/off with *left-clicks*.

Drawing outlines by entering coordinate units

When constructing a drawing in the screen just outlined, it can be assumed that each coordinate unit is equivalent to 1 millimetre when the drawing is printed or plotted full scale on an A3 sheet. This is because the limits of this screen are the same as the dimensions of an A3 sheet, which are 420 mm by 297 mm. There are two main methods of drawing outlines using coordinate units:

1. **Entering absolute units** – the x,y coordinate units positions of each corner of the outline are *entered* in response to prompts at the Command line.

2. **Entering relative units** – the x,y coordinate units distance between points on the outline are *entered* in response to prompts. Thus any point so *entered* is relative to the last point.

The Line tool

When any tool is called, the command line and the status line show a statement as to the action of the tool.

Left-click on the tool icon of the **Line** in the **Draw** toolbar or *enter* **l** at the command line. No matter which method is chosen, the prompts in the command window are similar.

Command: _line
Specify first point:

To start a drawing, in response to the **Specify first point:** prompt, *enter* the x,y coordinate units of the first point by typing the numbers at the keyboard with a comma between the x and y points. Then *right-click*, or press the *Return* key of the keyboard. The first prompt is then followed by the second prompt:
To point:

First example – absolute coordinate entry

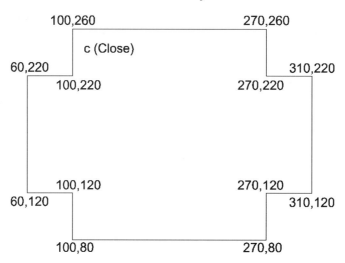

Command: _line
Specify first point: *enter* **100,260** *right-click*
Specify next point or [Undo]: *enter* **270,260** *right-click*
Specify next point or [Undo]: *enter* **270,220** *right-click*
Specify next point or [Close/Undo]: *enter* **310,220** *right-click*
Specify next point or [Close/Undo]: *enter* **310,120** *right-click*
Specify next point or [Close/Undo]: *enter* **270,120** *right-click*
Specify next point or [Close/Undo]: *enter* **270,80** *right-click*
Specify next point or [Close/Undo]: *enter* **100,80** *right-click*
Specify next point or [Close/Undo]: *enter* **100,120** *right-click*
Specify next point or [Close/Undo]: *enter* **60,120** *right-click*
Specify next point or [Close/Undo]: *enter* **60,220** *right-click*
Specify next point or [Close/Undo]: *enter* **100,220** *right-click*
Specify next point or [Close/Undo]: *enter* **c** *right-click*
Command:

Notes

1. Each time a new example is started, *enter* **z** and **Zoom** to **All** and set **Grid** to **10** and **Snap** to **5**.

2. If an error is made when *entering* figures, press **u** (for **Undo**). Pressing u repeatedly will eventually undo everything that has been added during a drawing session.

Second example – relative coordinate entry

When using relative coordinate entry, the symbol @ must be placed before the x,y coordinate units of the distance between the *entered* point and the last point on the outline.

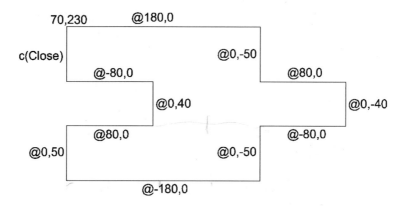

Command: _line
Specify first point: *enter* **70,230** *right-click*
Specify next point or [Undo]: *enter* **@180,0** *right-click*
Specify next point or [Undo]: *enter* **@0,-50** *right-click*
Specify next point or [Close/Undo]: *enter* **@80,0** *right-click*
Specify next point or [Close/Undo]: *enter* **@0,-40** *right-click*
Specify next point or [Close/Undo]: *enter* **@-80,0** *right-click*
Specify next point or [Close/Undo]: *enter* **@0,-50** *right-click*
Specify next point or [Close/Undo]: *enter* **@-180,0** *right-click*
Specify next point or [Close/Undo]: *enter* **@0,50** *right-click*
Specify next point or [Close/Undo]: *enter* **@80,0** *right-click*
Specify next point or [Close/Undo]: *enter* **@0,40** *right-click*
Specify next point or [Close/Undo]: *enter* **@-80,0** *right-click*
Specify next point or [Close/Undo]: *enter* **c (Close)** *right-click*
Command:

Notes

Some of the **x,y** coordinate units in this example are **+ve**, some **-ve**:

+ve x – horizontally to the right.

-ve x – horizontally to the left.

+ve y – vertically upwards.

-ve y – vertically downwards.

Third example – relative units involving angles

Command: _line
Specify first point: *enter* **70,190** *right-click*
Specify next point or [Undo]: *enter* **@50<45** *right-click*
Specify next point or [Undo]:: *enter* **@50<315** *right-click*
Specify next point or [Close/Undo]: *enter* **@70,0** *right-click*
Specify next point or [Close/Undo]: *enter* **@50<45** *right-click*
Specify next point or [Close/Undo]: *enter* **@50<315** *right-click*
Specify next point or [Close/Undo]: *enter* **@0,-60** *right-click*
Specify next point or [Close/Undo]: *enter* **@50<225** *right-click*
Specify next point or [Close/Undo]: *enter* **@50<135** *right-click*
Specify next point or [Close/Undo]: *enter* **@-70,0** *right-click*
Specify next point or [Close/Undo]: *enter* **@50<225** *right-click*
Specify next point or [Close/Undo]: *enter* **@50<135** *right-click*
Specify next point or [Close/Undo]: *enter* **c (Close)** *right-click*
Command:

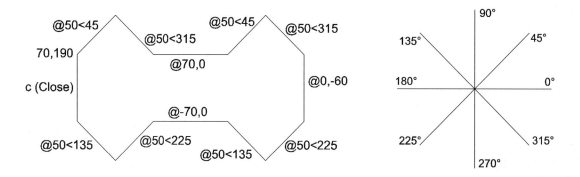

Angles in AutoCAD are measured counter-clockwise (anticlockwise) from East by default. This means that in the 360° of a circle, angles are measured as shown.

Notes

Assignments

To construct each of the assignments given in the drawings below, upon opening AutoCAD set **Limits** to **420,300** and **Zoom** to **All** before starting the construction each of the drawings. Do not include the dimensions – dimensioning is described in Chapter Three. Use the **Line** tool to construct the following drawings.

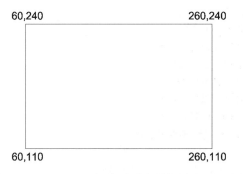

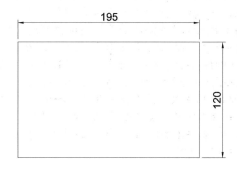

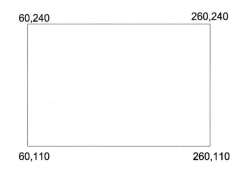

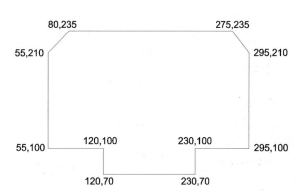

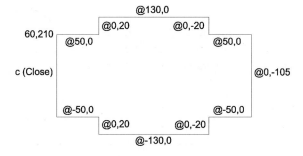

2 | Chapter Two

2D Drawing Procedures (Part 1)

The Polyline tool

The **Polyline** tool can be called either by selecting **Polyline** from the **Draw** drop-down menu, with a *left-click* on its tool icon in the **Draw** toolbar, or by *entering* **pl** or **pline** at the Command line. No matter which method is chosen, the prompts in the Command window are similar:

Command: _pline
Specify start point: *pick* or *enter* **coordinates**
Current line-width is 0
Specify next point or
[Arc/Halfwidth/Length/Undo/Width]:

Unless a simple straight polyline of zero width is required, it is necessary to respond with *entering* the initial letter of a prompt.

Polyline

PL
or
Pline

First example – polyline outline of Width 2

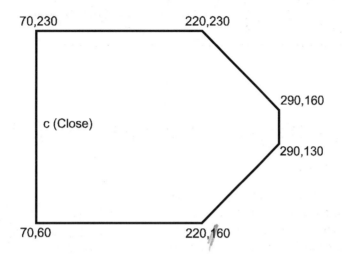

70,230   220,230

290,160

290,130

c (Close)

70,60   220,160

Command: _pline
Specify first point: *enter* **70,230** *right-click*
Current line-width is 0
Specify next point or [Arc/Halfwidth/Length/Undo/Width]: *enter* **w** *right-click*
Starting width <0>: *enter* **2** *right-click*
Ending width <2>: *right-click* **(accept the 2)**
Specify next point or [Arc/Close/Halfwidth/Length/Undo/Width]: *enter* **220,230**
right-click
Specify next point or [Arc/Close/Halfwidth/Length/Undo/Width]: *enter* **290,160**
right-click
Specify next point or [Arc/Close/Halfwidth/Length/Undo/Width]: *enter* **290,130**
right-click
Specify next point or [Arc/Close/Halfwidth/Length/Undo/Width]: *enter* **220,160**
right-click
Specify next point or [Arc/Close/Halfwidth/Length/Undo/Width]: *enter* **70,60**
right-click
Specify next point or [Arc/Close/Halfwidth/Length/Undo/Width]: *enter* **c (Close)**
right-click
Command:

Second example – polyline arcs

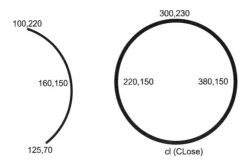

Command: _pline
Specify first point: *enter* **100,220** *right-click*
Current line-width is 0
Specify next point or [Arc/Halfwidth/Length/Undo/Width]: *enter* **w** *right-click*
Starting width <0>: *enter* **3** *right-click*
Ending width <3>: *right-click*
Specify next point or [Arc/Close/Halfwidth/Length/Undo/Width]: *enter* **a (Arc)**
right-click
Specify end point of arc or
[Angle/CEnter/CLose/Direction/Halfwidth/Line/Radius/Second pt/Undo/Width] *enter*
s (Second pt) *right-click*
Specify second point on arc: *enter* **160,150** *right-click*
Specify end point of arc: *enter* **125,70** *right-click*
Specify end point of arc or
[Angle/CEnter/Close/Direction/Halfwidth/Line/Radius/Second pt/Undo/Width]
right-click
Command: *right-click* **(back into pline sequence)**
PLINE
Specify first point: *enter* **220,150** *right-click*
Current line-width is 3
Specify next point or [Arc/Halfwidth/Length/Undo/Width]: *enter* **w** *right-click*
Starting width <0>: *enter* **5** *right-click*
Ending width <5>: *right-click*
Specify next point or [Arc/Close/Halfwidth/Length/Undo/Width]: *enter* **a (Arc)** *right-click*
Specify end point of arc or [Angle/CEnter/Direction/Halfwidth/Line/Radius/Second
pt/Undo/Width] *enter* **s (Second pt)** *right-click*
Specify second point on arc: *enter* **300,230** *right-click*
Specify end point of arc: *enter* **380,150** *right-click*
Specify end point of arc or
[Angle/CEnter/CLose/Direction/Halfwidth/Line/Radius/Second pt/Undo/Width] *enter*
cl (CLose) *right-click*
Command

Notes

The second example (right-hand drawing) describes the construction of a circle using the **Polyline** tool. If you use this method to construct a circle, care must be taken to *enter* or *pick* coordinate points at exact quadrant points for the circle.

Third example – differing polyline widths

In the upper example **Starting** and **Ending** widths are changed three times.

In the lower example **Starting width** and **Ending width** options are *entered* and the **Arc** and **Second pt** options are used.

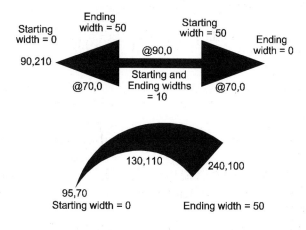

Fourth example – directional construction

When using either the **Line** or the **Polyline** tools, a "rubber band" from each specified point is attached to the point as the mouse is moved in any direction. If a length in units is *entered* at the keyboard, followed by a *right-click* a line forms at the keyed-in length along the direction taken by the rubber band. The arrows on the drawing show the direction taken by the mouse and hence the rubber band. This method of drawing is known as **tracking**.

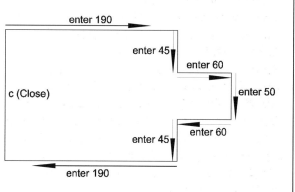

The Erase tool

Erase is a tool which will be frequently used. The tool can be used for erasing a single object, all objects within a window, or all objects crossed by a crossing window or fence.

The **Erase** tool can be called either with a *left-click* on its tool icon in the **Modify** toolbar, by *entering* **e** or **erase** at the command line, or by selecting **Erase** from the **Modify** drop-down menu. No matter which method is chosen, the prompts in the command window are similar. By far the easiest and quickest method of calling the tool is by *entering* **e** at the Command line followed by a *right-click*.

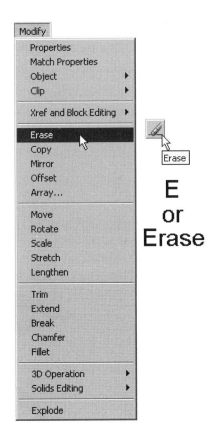

First example of the use of Erase

Command: _erase

Select objects: *pick* the object to be erased **1 found**

Select objects: *right-click*

Command: and the *picked* object is erased

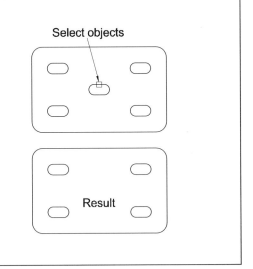

Second example of the use of Erase

Command: _crase

Select objects: *enter* w (Window) *right-click*

Specify first corner: *pick* **Specify opposite corner:** *pick* **5 found**

Select objects: *right-click*

Command: and all 5 objects within the window are erased

If the window is a crossing window, or if the **Specify first corner:** is *picked* at the bottom right of the objects to be erased and the **Specify opposite corner:** is *picked* top left, all the objects crossed by the lines of the crossing window are erased.

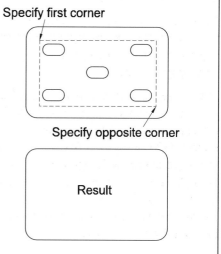

Specify first corner

Specify opposite corner

Result

Third example of the use of Erase

Command: _crase

Select objects: *enter* c (Crossing) *right-click*

Specify corner: *pick* **Specify opposite corner:** *pick*

Select objects: *right-click*

Command: and all objects crossed by the lines are erased.

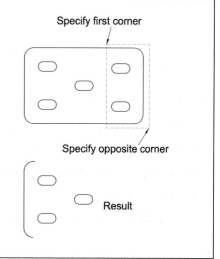

Specify first corner

Specify opposite corner

Result

Fourth example of the use of Erase

Another method of erasing objects crossed by lines is to use a **fence**.

Command: _erase

First fence point: *enter* f (fence) *right-click*

Specify corner: *pick*

Specify endpoint of line: *pick*

Specify endpoint of line: *pick*

Select objects: *right-click*

Command: and all objects crossed by the fence are erased.

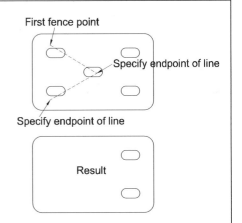

First fence point

Specify endpoint of line

Specify endpoint of line

Result

Object Snaps (osnaps)

Using object snaps (osnaps) allows the precise positioning of points in a drawing. Drawings can be accurately constructed by *snapping* objects to parts of other objects – to ends, to midpoints, to the intersections of objects etc. Osnaps can be set in a variety of ways, one of which is to *left-click* on the osnap icons from the **Object Snap** toolbar, brought on screen with a *right-click* in any toolbar and selecting the required osnap form the toolbar. When an osnap is selected from the toolbar, a prompt appears in the prompt line of the tool being used showing its abbreviation. As an example, when the **Snap to Endpoint** osnap is selected from the flyout, the prompt line shows:

Specify start point: _endp of

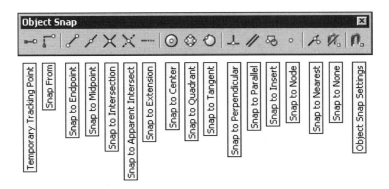

Notes

1. Osnaps can be *entered* at the command line to place a point in an exact position. The most frequently used osnap abbreviations are **end** – Endpoint; **mid** – Midpoint; **int** – Intersect; **cen** – Center; **qua** – Quadrant; **tan** – Tangent; and **per** – Perpendicular.

2. Osnaps can only be used when a tool is in action. If one is called when a tool is not in action the statement **Unknown command. Press F1 for help.** appears in the command window.

3. When an osnap is called a *pick* box appears at the intersection of the cursor hairs. A tool tip appears with the pick box.

First example of the use of osnaps

Examples of the osnaps **Snap to Endpoint**, **Snap to Midpoint**, **Snap to Intersection**, **Snap to Center** and **Snap to Quadrant**. The osnap *pick* boxes and tool tips are shown.

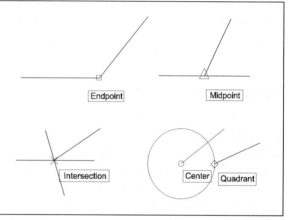

Second example of the use of osnaps

Examples of the osnaps **Snap to Tangent** and **Snap to Nearest**. The osnap *pick* boxes and tool tips are included in the illustration first example of the use of osnaps.

When the osnap **Object Snap Settings** is selected, the **Drafting Settings** dialog appears from which osnaps can be set if required.

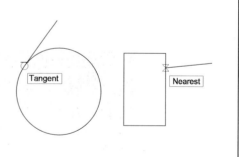

Saving drawings to file

It is advisable to save all the drawings constructed when working through this book to floppy disks, or to other forms of portable storage such as a Zip disk. Save your template file to your own floppy disk. Floppy disks will be in disk drive **a:**

The chapters in this book include a number of assignments. When these have been constructed, it is advisable to save the results to personal disks. Then you will be able to open any of your own drawings to add dimensions, or to recall at what stage you learned some new operation.

Save each assignment drawings to different directories. In the following examples **Unit02/** is the directory and **assign03.dwg** the file name.

Unit02/assign03.dwg

Unit02/assign06.dwg

To save drawings to file:

1. *Left-click* on **Save As…** in the **File** drop-down menu.

2. In the **Save Drawing As** dialog, select disk **a:**, followed by selecting the requisite chapter directory, then *enter* the file name in the **File Name** field.

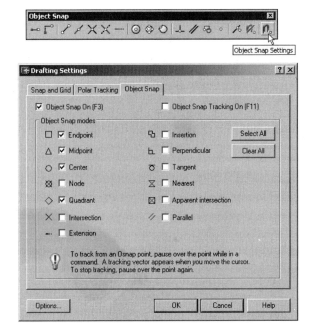

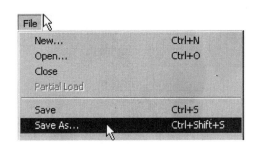

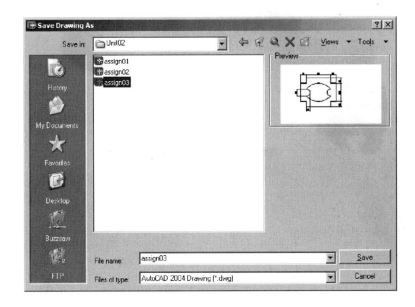

Assignments

To answer the assignments given by the six drawings below, set **Limits** to **420,300** and **Zoom** to **All**. Construct each of the drawings to the coordinate units or dimensions shown with the drawings. In order to be able to *enter* coordinates to construct the drawings some arithmetic on scrap paper may be necessary. The given dimensions are in coordinate units. Do not attempt to include the dimensions. Dimensioning is described later in this book. Use either the **Line** tool or the **Polyline** tool to complete the drawings. When using the **Polyline** tool, vary the width of the lines as indicated in the drawings.

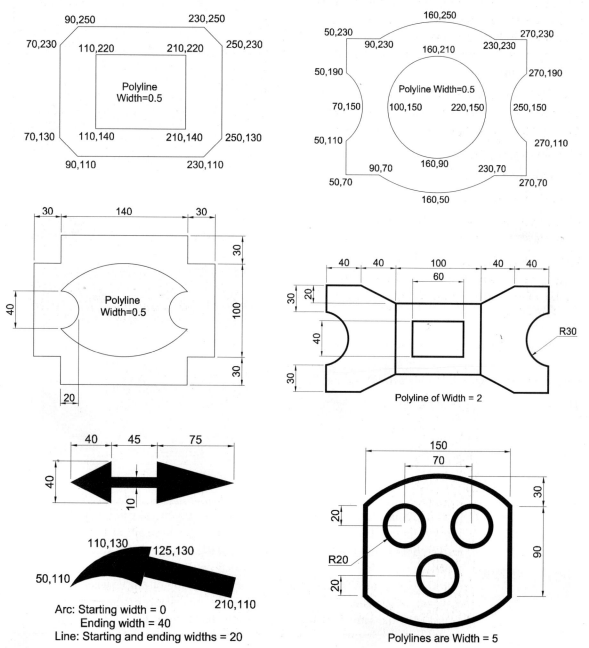

Drawing templates and drawing layouts

Most of the illustrations showing AutoCAD drawings in this book have been constructed in an AutoCAD drawing **template** set up within certain parameters. Details of the setting up of this template are given below. Once this template setup has been followed it is advisable to save the template as a file on disk as an AutoCAD drawing template (file extension ***.dwt**). The following settings are to be made:

Limits – lower left corner set to **0,0**; upper right corner set to **420,297**. An A3 sheet is 420 mm by 297 mm.

Units – set to **0** figures after the decimal point.

Grid – spacing set to **10**.

Snap spacing – set to **5**

Text Style – 2 text styles. **Arial** of height **6** and **Times New Roman** of height 10.

Dimension Style.

Layers – on which the following details are to be constructed:

0 – for outlines (the default AutoCAD layer).

Centre – for centre lines.

Construction – for construction lines.

Dimensions – for dimensions.

Hidden – for hidden lines.

Text – for text.

Limits

Enter **limits** at the command line and set the Upper Right Corner to 420,297. Remember to **Zoom** to **All** when limits have been set.

Units

At the command line: **Command**: enter **units** right-click.

The **Drawing Units** dialog appears. In the dialog *left-click* on the arrow to the right of the **Precision** field and again on **0** in the popup list which appears.

The *left-click* on the **OK** button of the dialog.

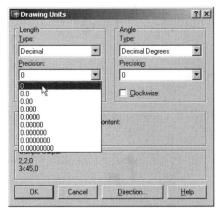

Grid and Snap

Set **Grid** to **10** and **Snap** to **5** as described on page 15.

Notes

Grid and Snap can be "toggled" on and off pressing the function keys **F7** (**Grid**) and **F9** (**Snap**). They can also be set on and off with *left-clicks* on the buttons marked **SNAP** and **GRID** in the status bar at the bottom of the AutoCAD window. When set on **Grid** shows as regularly spaced dots in the drawing area of the AutoCAD window. These grid dots assist in assessing distances when constructing drawings. When **Snap** is on movements of the cursor under mouse control are restricted to the setting of **Snap** horizontally and vertically.

Text Style

At the command line **Command**: *enter* **st** (or **style**) *right-click.* The **Text Style** dialog appears on screen. In thc dialog:

1. Select **ARIAL** from the popup list which appears with a *left-click* on the arrow of the **Font Name** field.

2. *Enter* **8** in the **Height** field.

3. *Left-click* on **New**. The name **Style1** appears in a **New Text Style** dialog. Overwrite that name with **ARIAL**. **ARIAL** then appears in the **Style Name** field.

4. *Left-click* on the **Apply** button and again on the **Accept** button and again on the **Close** button.

5. Repeat to set **Times New Roman** style of height **10**.

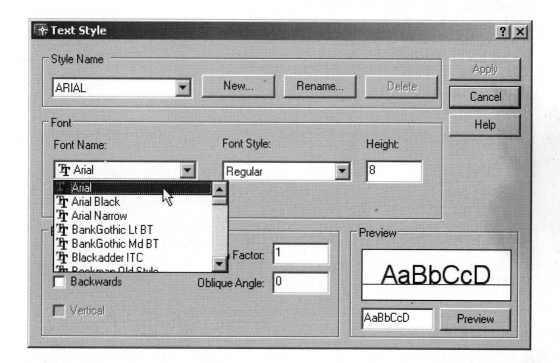

Dimension Style

1. At the command line:
   Command: *enter* **d** *right-click*
   The **Dimension Style Manager** dialog appears on screen. *Left-click* on the **Modify** button.

2. The **Modify Dimension Style: Standard** dialog appears. Note it has a number of tabs at the top of the dialog, a *left-click* on each of which will cause another dialog to appear.

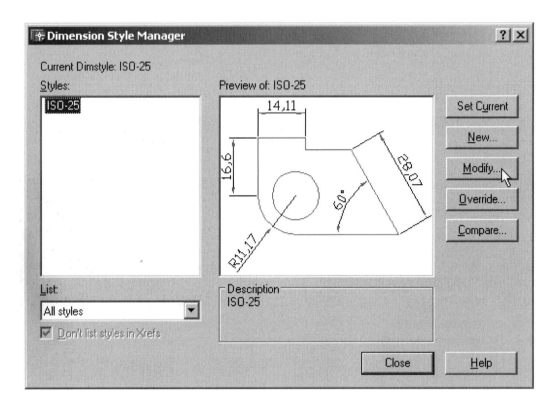

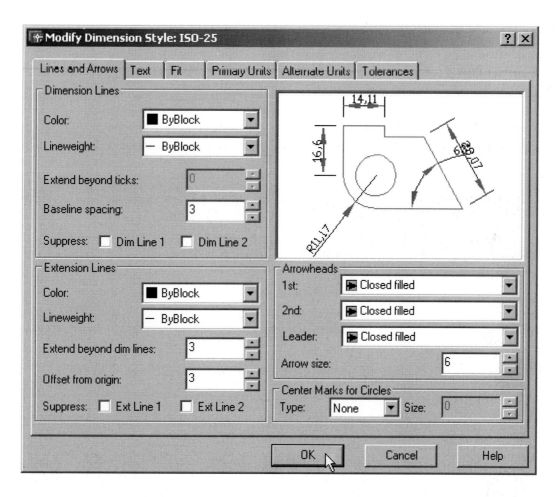

3. In the **Lines and Arrows** dialog, make settings as shown.

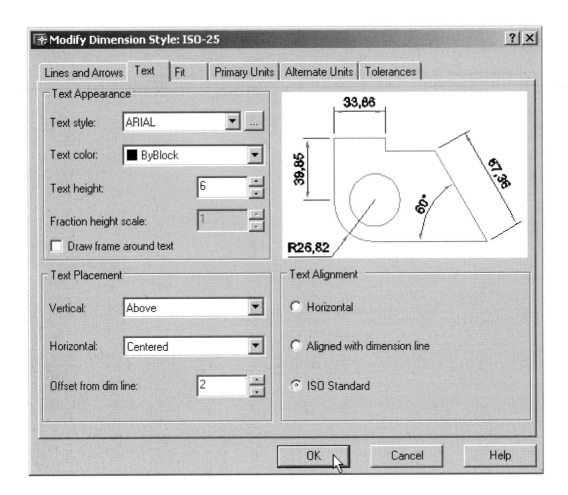

4. In the **Text** dialog make settings as shown.

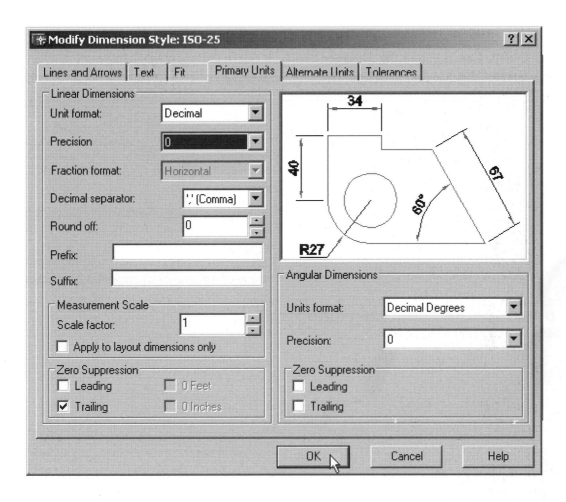

5. In the **Primary Units** dialog make settings as shown. *Left-click* the **OK** button. The **Dimension Style Manager** dialog reappears.

6. *Left-click* on the **New...** button. The **Create New Dimension Style** dialog appears. In the **New Style Name** field *enter* **A3_template** for the dimension style name. *Left-click* on the **Continue** button. The new name appears in the **Styles** list of the **Dimension Style Manager**. *Left-click* on the **Close** button.

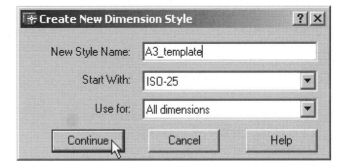

Layers

Left-click on the **Layers Properties Manager** icon in the **Layers** toolbar. The **Layer & Linetype Properties Manager** dialog appears. In the dialog:

1. *Left-click* on the **New** button 5 times to create 5 new layers **Layer1** to **Layer5**.

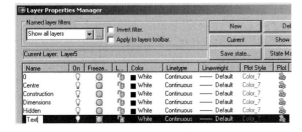

2. *Left-click* on each layer name in turn and overwrite the names for layers to:

   Centre
   Construction
   Dimensions
   Hidden
   Text

3. *Left-click* on **Continuous** in the **Centre** layer line. The **Select Linetype** dialog appears. In the dialog, *left-click* on **Load...** button.

4. The **Load or Reload** dialog appears, *Pick* **CENTER2** and *left-click* on **OK**. Then *pick* **HIDDEN2** and *left-click* on **OK**. Allocate **CENTER2** linetype to layer **Centre** and **HIDDEN2** to layer **Hidden**.

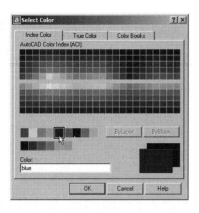

5. *Left-click* a colour box to the right of the layer name. The **Select Color** dialog appears. A colour for a layer can be set with a *left-click* on the colour required for each layer. Change the colour layers:

Centre – blue
Hidden – red
Dimensions – magenta
Text – grey (8)

6. Layers have now been set.

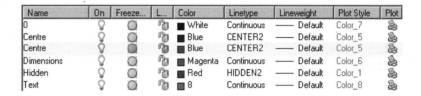

Name	On	Freeze...	L...	Color	Linetype	Lineweight	Plot Style	Plot
0	☿	○	ᵭ	■ White	Continuous	—— Default	Color_7	🖨
Centre	☿	○	ᵭ	■ Blue	CENTER2	—— Default	Color_5	🖨
Centre	☿	○	ᵭ	■ Blue	CENTER2	—— Default	Color_5	🖨
Dimensions	☿	○	ᵭ	■ Magenta	Continuous	—— Default	Color_6	🖨
Hidden	☿	○	ᵭ	■ Red	HIDDEN2	—— Default	Color_1	🖨
Text	☿	○	ᵭ	■ 8	Continuous	—— Default	Color_8	🖨

Linetype scale

When AutoCAD is first opened, the linetype scale will be set at 1 by default. When setting up this template the linetype scale will have to be changed to 30:

At the command line :

Command: *enter* **ltscale** *right-click*
Enter new LINETYPE scale factor <1.0000>: *enter* **30** *right-click*
Command:

Saving the template file

1. *Left-click* on **File** in the menu bar and in the **File** drop-down menu, *left-click* on **Save As...**. The **Save Drawing As** dialogue box appears.

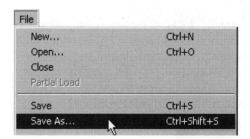

2. *Left-click* in the **Files of type:** field and select **Drawing Template File (*.dwt)** from the popup list which appears.

3. In the **File name:** field *enter* **A3_template** and the name to which the template file is to be saved.

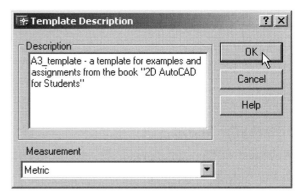

4. *Left-click* on the **Save** button. The **Template Description** dialogue box appears. In the **Description** box enter a suitable description for your template such as is shown in the illustration.

5. Next time AutoCAD is loaded the template can now be opened before commencing work on examples and assignments.

An A3 drawing layout

Borders and a title block could be added to this template if desired. Details of a suitable border and title block are shown. The outlines are polylines of a width of **0.7**. The name **2D AutoCAD** is in the **Times New Roman** text style of height **10**. The other text in the title block are in the **Arial** style of height **6**.

Saving the drawing layout

Save the drawing as a template with the name **A3_layout.dwt**. This means that in the **Files of type** field **AutoCAD drawing Template File (*.dwt)** must first be selected from the **Files of type** popup list before the template can be saved.

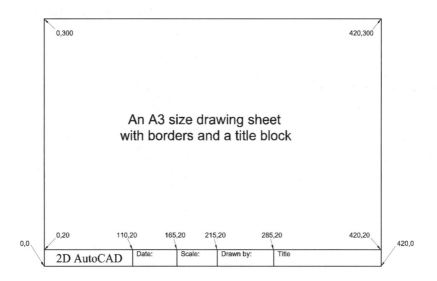

An A3 size drawing sheet
with borders and a title block

| 2D AutoCAD | Date: | Scale: | Drawn by: | Title |

An A4 template

To prepare a template suitable for drawings to be plotted full size on an A4 sheet:

■ **Limits** – lower left corner set to **0,0**; upper right corner set to **297,210**. An A4 sheet is 297 mm by 210 mm.

■ **Units** – set to **0** figures after the decimal point.

■ **Grid** – spacing set to **10**.

■ **Snap spacing** – set to **5**

■ **Text Style** – 2 text styles. **Simplex** (renamed **MAIN**) of height **2.5** and **Italic** of height 5.5.

■ **Dimension Style** – arrows 2.5. Text **MAIN** 2.5.

■ **Layers** – on which the following details are to be constructed:

   ■ **0** – for outlines (the default AutoCAD layer).

   ■ **CENTRE** – for centre lines. Linetype **CENTER2**. Colour **RED**.

   ■ **PSVPORTS** – for outlines of viewports. Linetype **CONTINUOUS**. Colour **CYAN**.

   ■ **HATCH** – for hatchings. Linetype **CONTINUOUS**. Colour **GREEN**.

   ■ **TITLE** – for border and title. Linetype **CONTINUOUS**. Colour **MAGENTA**.

   ■ **Linetype Scale** – set to **15**.

Save the template to the name **A4_template.dwt**.

An A4 drawing layout

1. *Left-click* the arrow on the right of the **Layers** field and in the popup list which appears, *left-click* on the layer name **TITLE** to make that layer the current.

2. Construct borders:

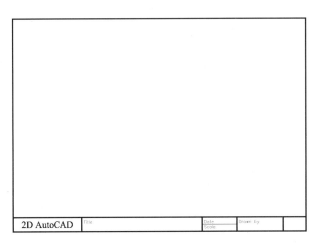

2D AutoCAD	Title		Date	Drawn by
			Scale	

Command: *enter* **pl (polyline)** *right-click*
Specify start point: *enter* **5,5** *right-click*
Specify next point or [Arc/Halfwidth/Length/Undo/Width]: *enter* **w (Width)** *right-click*
Specify starting width <0>: *enter* **1** *right-click*
Specify ending width <1>: *right-click*
Specify next point or [Arc/Halfwidth/Length/Undo/Width]: *enter* **5,185** *right-click*
Specify next point or [Arc/Halfwidth/Length/Undo/Width]: *enter* **260,185** *right-click*
Specify next point or [Arc/Halfwidth/Length/Undo/Width]: *enter* **260,5** *right-click*
Specify next point or [Arc/Halfwidth/Length/Undo/Width]: *enter* **c (Close)** *right-click*
Command: *right-click*
Specify start point: *enter* **5,17** *right-click*
Specify next point or [Arc/Halfwidth/Length/Undo/Width]: *enter* **260,17** *right-click*
Command:
  Then construct plines between coordinates **65,5** and **65,17**; **170,5** and **170,17**; **200,5** and **200,17**; **240,5** and **240,17**.

3. Add text in the spaces within the title block using the text style **MAIN** and the text style **Times New Roman** to produce the result as shown.

4. Save the screen as a template with the title **A4_template.dwt**.

Short cut keys

When working with AutoCAD many of the operations involved can be carried out by using short-cut keys or by *entering* abbreviations for a tool. Examples of tool abbreviations have already been given **l** for **Line** and **pl** for **Pline**. When working in relative coordinates pressing the keyboard keys **Ctrl+D** will change the coordinate numbers showing at the left-hand end of the status bar from absolute coordinates

(**35,90,0**) to relative coordinates (**95<45,0**). Other short-cut keys will be seen in the drop-down menus. The short-cut keys from the **File** drop-down are shown.

Assignments

1. From the **File** drop-down menu select **New…** and in the **AutoCAD Today** dialog, *left-click* on the **Create Drawings** tab and from the file list *left-click* on the name **A3_template.dwt**. When the template opens on screen construct the drawings as shown:

   ■ Drawing 1: Use the **Line** tool to construct the outline.

   ■ Drawing 2: Use the **Polyline** tool set to **Width** of **0.3**.

   ■ Drawing 3: Use the **Polyline** tool set to **Width** of **1**.

   ■ Drawing 4; use the **Polyline** tool set to a **Width** of **2**.

2. From the **File** drop-down menu select **New…** and in the **AutoCAD Today** dialog, *left-click* on the **Create Drawings** tab and from the file list *left-click* on the name **A4_layout.dwt**. When the template opens on screen construct the drawings as shown:

   ■ Drawing 1: Use the **Line** tool to construct the outline.

   ■ Drawing 2: Use the **Polyline** tool set to **Width** of **0.3**.

   ■ Drawing 3: Use the **Polyline** tool set to **Width** of **1**.

   ■ Drawing 4: Use the **Polyline** tool set to a **Width** of **2**.

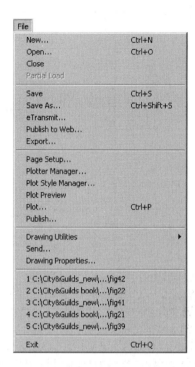

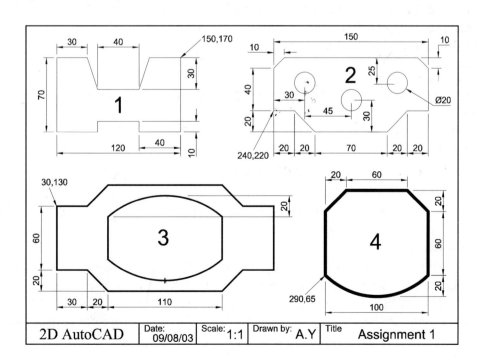

43

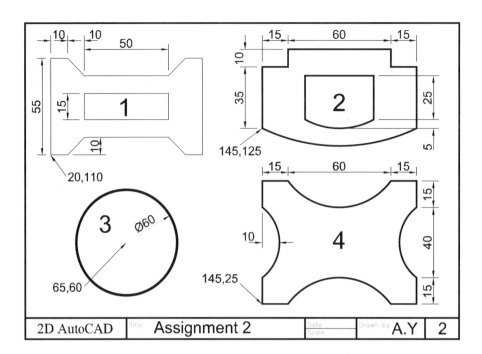

| 2D AutoCAD | Title | Assignment 2 | Date / Scale | Drawn by A.Y | 2 |

The Zoom tools

Zoom tools are important. You will be using them repeatedly. There are several methods of calling the tool – from the **Zoom** toolbar, or by *entering* z (or **zoom**) at the command line. The quickest method is to *enter* z at the command line, followed by *entering* the initial letter of the option for the type of zoom required.

Command: *enter* **z** *right-click*
All/Center/Dynamic/Extents/Previous/Scale/Window/<realtime>:

The options most likely to be used most often are **<realtime>**, **Window** and **Previous**. In practise, **<realtime>** and **Window** have the same result – selecting part of a drawing to be zoomed and so fill the Drawing area of the AutoCAD window. The **Previous** zoom causes the drawing to reappear as it was before using **Window**. Practise with the other prompts of the **Zoom** sequence in order to understand how they work.

The Pan tool and Aerial View window

Left-click on **Aerial View** in the **View** drop-down menu. The **Aerial View Window** appears at the bottom right corner of the AutoCAD window. It holds a miniature view of the full drawing area and the part of the drawing on screen is enclosed by a thick black line rectangle in the **Aerial View**. The **Aerial View Window** is of particular value when working with large drawings in screens with **Limits** set to large numbers, because it shows clearly the part of the whole drawing which is being worked at the time. Call the **Pan** tool by *entering* p at the Command line:

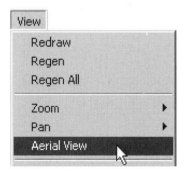

Command: *enter* **p** *right-click* **and a pan hand icon appears on screen.**
PAN
Press ESC or ENTER to exit, or right-click to activate popup menu

Moving the mouse *drags* the drawing on screen in the direction in which the pan icon is moved. This allows work in areas on part of a drawing not currently on screen when constructing very large drawings. *Right-click* and a popup menu appears. *Left-click* on **Exit** in this menu and the panning ends. A black line rectangle in the **Aerial View Window** shows that part of the drawing which is on screen. When using **Zoom**, the black line rectangle surrounds the area zoomed on screen.

Text

The Text Style dialog

It is necessary to first determine the text font and text size to be used before text can be included in a drawing. AutoCAD includes a large variety of different text fonts. Two types of text fonts are available in AutoCAD – Window True Text fonts (TT) and AutoCAD (SHX).

The settings for a font to be used are made in the **Text Style** dialog, called to screen either with a *left-click* on **Text Style** in the **Format** drop-down menu or by *entering* **st** at the command line.

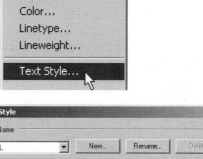

In the **Text Style** dialog, which then appears, to set a text font as current, *left-click* on the arrow to the right of the **Font Name** field and select a font name from the scrollable popup list which appears. In the example shown, **ARIAL** (a Windows TT font) has been selected. **ARIAL** appears in the **Font Name** field. *Left-click* on the **New...** button of the dialog and the **New Text Style** dialog appears. *Enter* the name **ARIAL** in the **Style Name** field and *left-click* on the **OK** button.

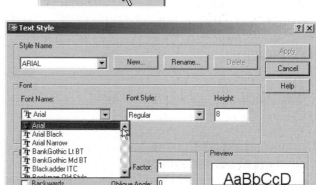

Then *enter* the required height in the **Height** field of the **Text Style** dialog. Finally *left-click* on the **Apply** button and on the **Close** button and the font is set.

Set several fonts in this manner. To see which fonts have been set, *left-click* on the arrow at the right of the **Style Name** field and the fonts so set are displayed in a popup list.

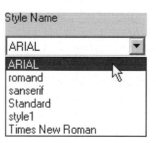

Notes

In the **Text Style** dialogue box:

1. The appearance of the selected font shows in the **Preview** field.

2. The **Height** of the selected font is set by *entering* figures in the **Height** field.

3. **Width** and **Obliquing Angle** of the selected font can be set in the respective fields.

4. If a Windows True Text font is chosen, its style can be set from the popup list appearing with a *left-click* on the arrow to the right of the **Font Style** field.

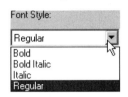

Text tools

There are two methods of calling text tools – **Multiline Text** (mtext) and **Single Line Text** (dynamic text or dtext).

To call **Multiline Text**, *left-click* its tool icon in the **Draw** or *left-click* its name in the **Text** sub-menu of the **Draw** drop-down menu, or *enter* **t** at the command line.

To call **Single Line Text** *left-click* its tool icon in the **Draw** or *left-click* its name in the **Text** sub-menu of the **Draw** drop-down menu, or *enter* **dt** at the command line.

First example – Multiline Text

1. Call Mtext.

Command:_mtext Current text style: "ARIAL" Text height: 8
Specify first corner: *pick* **or** *enter* **coordinates**
Specify opposite corner or [Height/Justify/Line spacing/Rotate/Style/Width]: *pick* **or** *enter* **coordinates**

2. The **Text Formatting** dialog appears.

3. *Enter* required text in the window, now under the dialog.

4. *Left-click* the **OK** button. The text appears in the area *picked* by the **first** and **opposite** corners.

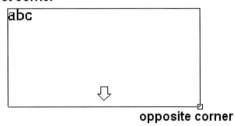

first corner

abc

opposite corner

1. As shown, if the text style is a Windows True Type font the text can be amended to **Bold**, *Italic* or <u>Underlined</u> or a combination of these.

2. If the text style is an AutoCAD SHX style, these amendments cannot take place.

Second example – Single Line Text

Call **Single Line Text**;

Command: *enter* **dt** *right-click*
Command:_mtext Current text style: "ARIAL" Text height: 8
Specify start point of text or [Justify/Style]: *pick* or *enter* **coordinates**
Specify rotation of text <0>: *right-click*

Enter text: *enter* the required text

The text as *entered* appears directly on screen. Pressing the **Return** key allows a second line of text to be *entered*. A second press of the **Return** key and the command line shows:

Command:

1. When using the **Dtext** tool **Single Line Text**, a *right-click* to move text down to the next line must be replaced by pressing the **Return** key of the keyboard. Similarly a second pressing of the **Return** ends the use of the tool. *Right-clicks* produce no response in this case.

2. When using the **Dtext** tool for adding text to a drawing, symbols can be included by *entering* the following:

   %%d – degree symbol. Thus **45%%d** and **45°** will appear on screen.

   %%c – diameter symbol. Thus **%%c45** and **Ø45** will appear on screen.

   %%p – tolerance symbol. Thus **45%%p0.5** and **45±0.5** will appear on screen.

   %%u – underscore. Thus **%%u45** and <u>45</u> will appear on screen.

Text Styles

A sample of Windows True Type fonts and AutoCAD SHX fonts is shown in an illustration.

Windows True Type fonts

Arial Regular Height 8

Arial Black Bold Height 14

LotusLineDraw Regular
Height 12

Times New Roman Bold Italic Height 12

Sans Serif Regular Height 12

AutoCAD SHX fonts

Gothicc.shx Height 15

Italic.shx Height 15

Romanc.shxHeight 10

Checking spelling

At the command line:

Command: *enter* **ddedit** *right-click*

Select an annotation object: *pick* the text with mis-spellings

The **Text Edit** dialog appears with the selected text in its **Text** field. Amend the text using normal word processing methods, followed by a *click* on the **OK button.**

Select an annotation object: *right-click*

Command:

The corrected text appears in place of the mis-spelt text.

This texxt has been spellt incorrectly

This text has been spelt correctly

Assignments

1. **Open** the **A3_template.dwt** template. Set the text style to **Courier Bold** of **Height=10**. Place the following text anywhere in the drawing area of the screen:

    The circle is **Ø75.5±0.5.**
    <u>Bolt 100 x M15</u>
    The angle of the two lines must be exactly 60°
    The tolerance for all dimensions is to be **±0.5**

2. While still in the A3_template.dwt add the following sentence six times:

This text is in the ———— style of a height —
Where ———— is the name of a text style and — is the figure for the chosen text height. Use six different fonts of differing heights.

3. Working in any text style regarded as being suitable, place the following sentence twice in the drawing area:

   The spilling of thet ext must be chekked becase it contins several spalling miistakes.

Check the spelling and correct the sentence.

4. **Open** any one of the drawings, examples or assignments from previous chapters and practise using the **Zoom** tools on the drawing. Or construct the given drawing in an A3_template.dwt and practise on that.

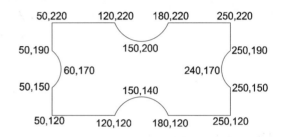

5. Practise using **Zoom** window, **Zoom** All, **Zoom** Previous, **Zoom** Scale, **Zoom** Dynamic and **Zoom** Center on the drawing.

6. Practise using the **Pan** tool on the drawing.

7. With the drawing still on screen, call the **Aerial View** window and practice using the **Zoom** and **Pan** tools, noting the results in the **Aerial Zoom** window as you do so.

8. Construct the drawing given below in an A3_template.dwt. Open the **Aerial View** window. Call the **Zoom** tool and practise using the tool on the drawing you have constructed.

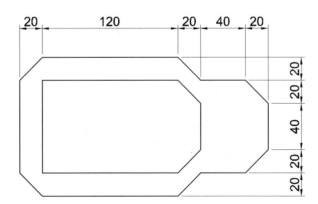

3 | Chapter Three

2D drawing procedures (Part 2)

AutoSnap

Enter **options** at the command line and the **Options** dialog appears.

In the dialog, *left-click* on the **Drafting** label. A sub-dialog appears. In the **AutoSnap Settings** area of this dialog, *left-click* in each of the check boxes to set them all on. There are four parts of AutoSnap when it is set to be in action: A **Marker**, a **Magnet** a **Snap Tip** and an **Aperture** box.

1. If the marker is turned off no pick box appears with the AutoSnap.

2. If the magnet is turned off, AutoSnap does not lock to the nearest snap point.

3. If the snap tip is turned off it doesn't show when osnaps are selected.

4. If the aperture box is turned off no aperture box appears when osnaps are selected.

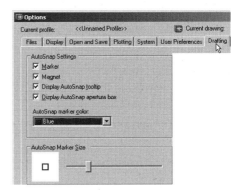

Notes

1. If several osnaps are set on in the **Drafting** dialog, when AutoSnap is active, pressing the **Tab** key of the keyboard will toggle through all the possible snap points one after the other.

2. A different shape marker will show for each of the AutoSnap markers, depending upon which is in use.

3. AutoSnap only functions for osnaps already selected or set.

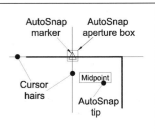

The Circle tool

To call the **Circle** tool, either *left-click* on the **Circle** tool icon in the **Draw** toolbar, or on **Circle** from the **Draw** drop-down menu, or *enter* **c** or **circle** at the command line. When calling the tool from the **Draw** drop-down menu a sub-menu appears from which prompts from the tool's sequence can be selected instead of *entering* the prompt initials at the command line.

First example – with osnap and AutoSnap on

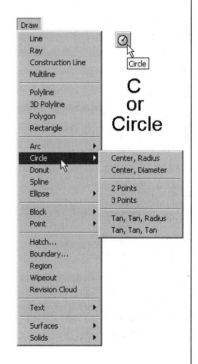

Command: _circle
Specify center point for circle or [3P/2P/Ttr (Tan tan radius]: *enter* **80,200** *right-click*
Specify radius of circle or [Diameter]: *enter* **50** *right-click*
Command: *enter* **l (Line)** *right-click*
Specify first point: *pick* **near the top of R50 circle**
Specify next point or [Undo]: *drag* **to the right** *enter* **140** *right-click*
Specify next point or [Undo]: *pick* **the end of the line**
Specify next point or [Close/Undo]: *pick* **the R30 circle and then near its centre**
Specify next point or [Close/Undo]: *right-click*
Command: *right-click*
LINE Specify first point: *pick* **R50 circle and then near its centre**
Specify next point or [Undo]: *pick* **the lower part of the R30 circle**
Specify next point or [Close/Undo]:
Command:

First example – using the Ttr prompt

Command: _circle
Specify center point for circle or [3P/2P/Ttr (Tan tan radius]: *enter* **t (Ttr)** *right-click*

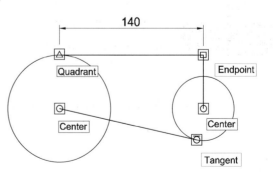

Second example – examples using Ttr prompt

Specify point on object for first tangent of circle: *pick*
Specify point on object for second tangent of circle: *pick*
Specify radius of circle or [Diameter]: *enter* **40** *right-click*
Command:

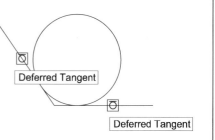

Third example – using the 3P and 2P prompts

Command: _circle

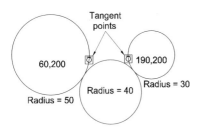

Specify center point for circle or [3P/2P/Ttr (Tan tan radius)]: *enter* **3p** *right-click*
Specify first point on circle: *enter* **80,170** *right-click*
Specify second point on circle: *enter* **140,20** *right-click*
Specify third point on circle: *enter* **180,140** *right-click*
Command: *right-click*
Specify center point for circle or [3P/2P/Ttr (Tan tan radius)]: *enter* **2p** *right-click*
Specify first end point of circle's diameter: *enter* **90,190** *right-click*
Specify second end point of circle's diameter: *enter* **190,150** *right-click*
Command:

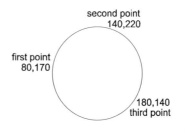

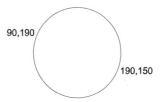

The Arc tool

To call the **Arc** tool, either *left-click* on the **Arc** tool icon in the **Draw** toolbar, or on **Arc** from the **Draw** drop-down menu, or *enter* **a** or **arc** at the command line. When calling the tool from the **Draw** drop-down menu a sub-menu appears from which prompts from the tool's sequence can be selected instead of *entering* the prompt initials at the command line.

The examples shown below were all drawn after selection from the **Arc** sub-menu from the **Draw** drop-down menu, but the capital letters of the prompts could have been *entered* instead.

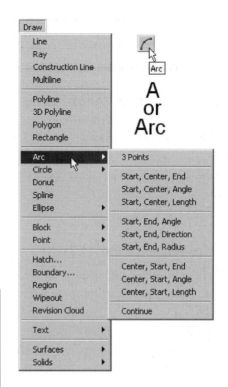

When drawing arcs they must be drawn anticlockwise (counter-clockwise).

First example – 3 Points

Command: _arc Specify start point of arc or [Center] *pick* **a point**
Specify second point of arc or [Center/End]: *pick* **a point**
Specify end point of arc: *pick* **a point**
Command:

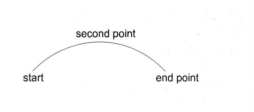

Second example – Start, Center, End

Command: _arc Specify start point of arc or [Center] *pick* **a point**
Specify second point of arc or [Center/End]:_c
Specify center of arc: *pick* **a point**
Specify end point of arc or [Angle/Chord/Length: *pick* **a point**
Command:

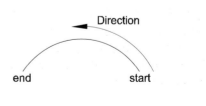

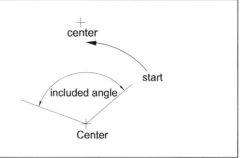

Third example – Start, Center, Angle

**Command: _arc Specify start point of arc
or [Center]** *pick* **a point
Specify end point of arc or [Angle/chord
Length]:_a Specify included angle:** *enter*
120 *right-click*
Command:

center

center

start

included angle

Center

The Edit Polyline (Pedit) tool

Polylines (plines) can be edited with the aid of the **Edit Polyline** tool, usually referred to as **Pedit**. The easiest method of calling **Pedit** is to *enter* **pe** at the command line, which then shows:

Command: *enter* **pe** *right-click*
PEDIT Select polyline or [Multiple]: *pick*
Enter an option [Close/Join/Width/Edit vertex/ Fit/Spline/Decurve/Lt gen/Undo]:

First example – using the Close prompt

Construct a polyline of width =1 similar to that given in the left-hand drawing. Call **pedit**:

Command: *enter* **pe** *right-click*
PEDIT Select polyline or [Multiple]: *pick*
Enter an option [Close/Join/Width/Edit vertex/ Fit/Spline/Decurve/Lt gen/Undo]:
enter **c** *right-click*
Enter an option [Open/Join/Width/Edit vertex/ Fit/Spline/Decurve/Lt gen/Undo]:
right-click
Command:

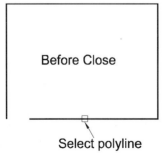

Before Close

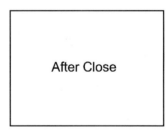

After Close

Select polyline

Second example – using the Width prompt

Construct a simple polyline rectangle of width = 0 (left-hand drawing). Copy twice. Change the width of one of the copies to a width = 2 (central drawing) and the other to a width = 10 (right-hand drawing). To change the widths of the two polylines:

Command: *enter* **pe** *right-click*
PEDIT Select polyline or [Multiple]: *pick*
Enter an option [Close/Join/Width/Edit vertex/ Fit/Spline/Decurve/Lt gen/Undo]: *enter* **w** *right-click*
Specify width for all segments: *enter* **5** *right-click*
Enter an option [Open/Join/Width/Edit vertex/ Fit/Spline/Decurve/Lt gen/Undo]: *right-click*
Command:

Width = 0	Width = 5	Width = 10

Third example – using the Multiple prompt

Construct four plines such as those shown – the first is a straight pline, the second an arc, the third a closed triangle and the fourth straight plines joined to an arc. To change the width of all plines:

Command: *enter* **pe** *right-click*
PEDIT Select polyline or [Multiple]: *enter* **m** *right-click*
Select objects: *pick* **first pline 1 found**
Select objects: *pick* **second pline 1 found, 2 total**
Select objects: *pick* **third pline 1 found, 3 total**
Select objects: *pick* **fourth pline 1 found, 4 total**
Select objects: *right-click*
Enter an option [Close/Join/Width/Edit vertex/ Fit/Spline/Decurve/Lt gen/Undo]: *enter* **w** *right-click*
Specify width for all segments: *enter* **8** *right-click*
Enter an option [Open/Join/Width/Edit vertex/ Fit/Spline/Decurve/Lt gen/Undo]: *right-click*
Command:

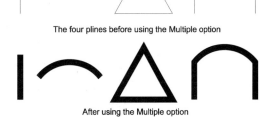

The four plines before using the Multiple option

After using the Multiple option

Fourth example – Using pedit on circles

If an arc is acted upon by **Polyline Edit**, the following appears at the command line:

Command: *enter* pe *right-click*
PEDIT Select polyline or [Multiple]: *pick* the arc
Object selected is not a polyline
Do you want to change it into one? (Y): *right-click*
Enter an option [Close/Join/Width/Edit vertex/ Fit/Spline/Decurve/Lt gen/Undo]:
right-click
Command:

and the arc changes to a pline.

To change a circle into a pline, it must first be changed to an arc by using the **Break** command:

Command: *enter* br (Break) *right-click*
BREAK Select object: *pick* a point on the circle
Specify second break point or [First]: *pick* a second point counter-clockwise to the first point
Command:

and the circle breaks as indicated in the central drawing. Now call **Pedit**:

Command: *enter* pe *right-click*
PEDIT Select polyline or [Multiple]: *pick* the arc
Object selected is not a polyline
Do you want to change it into one? (Y): *right-click* and the circle changes to a pline
Enter an option [Close/Join/Width/Edit vertex/ Fit/Spline/Decurve/Lt gen/Undo]:
enter **w** *right-click*
Specify width for all segments: *enter* 10 *right-click*
Enter an option [Open/Join/Width/Edit vertex/ Fit/Spline/Decurve/Lt gen/Undo]:
right-click
Command:

Circle   After Break   Width=10

Assignments

To construct the assignments that follow, use the tools **Line**, **Polyline**, **Circle**, **Arc** and **Edit Polyline** and work in **A3_template.dwt** templates. More accurate drawings will be possible if osnaps and AutoSnap are freely used when constructing the answers. Do not include any of the dimensions.

1. Construct the given outline using the **Polyline** tool and working to a Width = **1**.

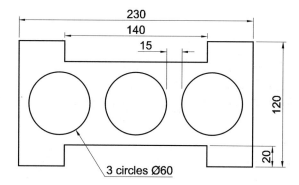

2. Draw three lines as shown (**Line** tool). Add the circles with the aid of the **Tan tan radius** prompt of the **Circle** tool sequence. Use **Pedit** to set the circle widths to **1**.

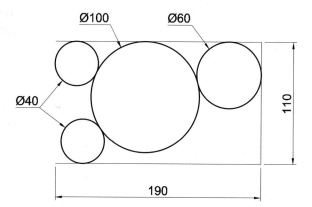

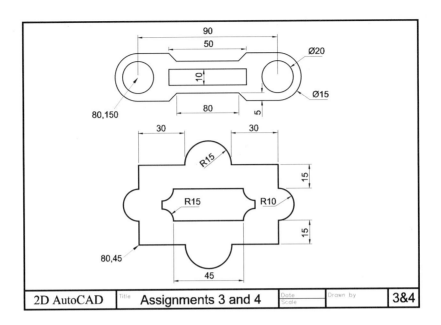

| 2D AutoCAD | Title **Assignments 3 and 4** | Date | Drawn by | **3&4** |
| | | Scale | | |

3. Open the template **A4_template.dwt** and within its borders construct the given outline (upper drawing) using the **Polyline** tool to a Width = **0.7**.

4. Within the template on which assignment **3** has been drawn add the given outline (lower drawing) to a width of **1.5** using the **Polyline** tool.

5. The pictorial drawing shows a shelf mounted on two wall supports.

The other drawing shows a dimensioned view of one of the supports. Construct this drawing of the support using plines to a Width of **1**.

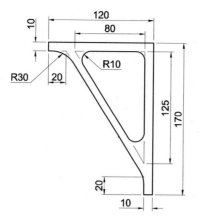

6. Two pictorial views of a simple engineering component are given, one from the rear, the other from the front.

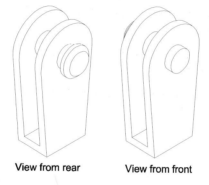

View from rear   View from front

The other drawing shows a two-view orthographic projection of the component. Ignoring the hidden detail lines, construct a copy of the two views using the **Polyline** tool working to a width of **0.7**.

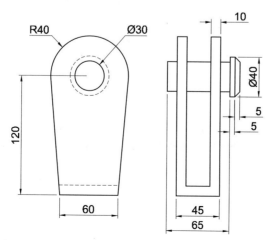

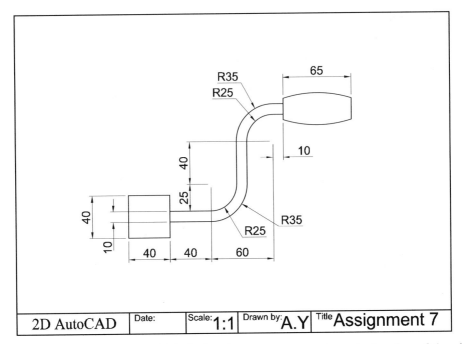

| 2D AutoCAD | Date: | Scale: 1:1 | Drawn by: A.Y | Title Assignment 7 |

7. Open the template **A3_layout** and within its borders construct an accurate drawing of the given handle working to a width of **0.7**.

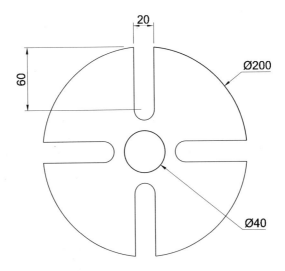

8. Construct an accurate copy of the given drawing, with **Polyline** set to a width of **0.7**.

The Polygon tool

The **Polygon** tool can be called with a *left-click* on its tool icon in the **Draw** toolbar, or with a *left-click* on its name in the **Draw** drop-down menu, or by entering **pol** or **polygon** at the command line. When called, the command line shows:

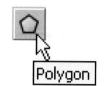

Command: _polygon Enter number of sides <4>:

Example – a variety of polygons

Command: _polygon Enter number of sides <4>: *enter* **6** *right-click*
Specify center of polygon or [Edge]: *enter* **110,230** *right-click*
Enter an option [Inscribed in circle/Circumscribed about circle] <I>: *right-click*
Specify radius of circle: *enter* **60** *right-click*
Command:

Open the **A3_template.dwt** template and draw polygons as shown.

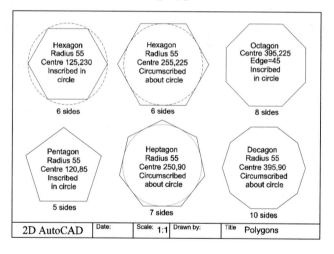

The Ellipse tool

The **Ellipse** tool can be called with a *left-click* on its tool icon in the **Draw** toolbar, from or with a *left-click on* its name in the **Draw** drop-down menu, or by *entering* **el** or **ellipse** at the command line. When called, the command line shows:

Command _ellipse
Specify axis endpoint of elliptical arc or [Center]:

Example – a variety of ellipses

Open the **A3_template.dwt** and call the **Ellipse** tool:

Command _ellipse
Specify axis endpoint of elliptical arc or
[Center]: *enter* **c (Center)** *right-click*
Specify center of ellipse: *enter* **270,210**
right-click
Specify endpoint of axis: *enter* **330,210**
right-click
Specify distance to other axis or
[Rotation]: *enter* **210,210** *right-click*
Command:

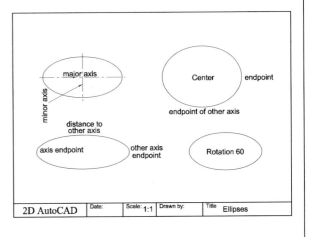

1. The longer axis of an ellipse is its **major axis**. The shorter is its **minor axis**.

2. Ellipses can be constructed as true ellipses or as plines. Call the set variable **PELLIPSE**. If this variable is set to 0 ellipses will be true. If set to 1, ellipses plines.

   Command: *enter* **pellipse** *right-click*
   Enter new value for PELLIPSE <0>: *enter* **1** *right-click*
   Command:

3. An ellipse may be seen as a circle which has been rotated around its horizontal diameter. As the rotation increases, so the vertical diameter of the circle becomes smaller and what appears as an ellipse is seen. The **Rotation** option asks for the angle through which the rotation has taken place to be *entered*.

The Rectangle tool

The **Rectangle** tool can be called either with a *left-click* on its tool icon in the **Draw** toolbar, from its name in the **Draw** drop-down menu, or by *entering* **rec** or **rectang** at the command line. When called, the command line shows:

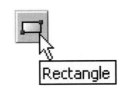

Command:_rectang
Specify first corner point or [Chamfer/Elevation/Fillet/Thickness/Width]:
pick or *enter* **coords**
Specify other corner point or [Dimensions]: *pick* or *enter* **coords**
Command:

First example – a variety of rectangles

30,240

Entering coordinates

130,175

Chamfer=15

Using Chamfer option

Fillet=20

Using Fillet option

Width=5

Using Width option

Chamfer=10
Width=10

Using Chamfer and
width options

Length=90
Width=50

Using Dimension
option - length and
width

Second example – the Elevation option

When the **Elevation** option is used, the
rectangle is constructed at the height above the
x,y plane as indicated by the figures *entered* in
response to:

Specify the elevation for rectangles <0>:
enter **60**

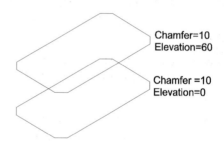

Chamfer=10
Elevation=60

Chamfer =10
Elevation=0

Transparent commands

When working with any tool, zooms can be called by taking advantage of being able to call zoom or pan
as transparent command by *entering* an apostrophe before the tool name or its abbreviation at the
command line – for example: of **'z** or **'zoom**. After zooming (or panning), the interrupted command is
resumed. As an example, when constructing an ellipse:

Command: *enter* **el** *right-click*
Specify axis endpoint of ellipse or [Arc/Center]; *pick*
Specify other endpoint of ellipse: *pick*
Specify distance to other axis or [Rotation]: *enter* **'z** *right-click*
>>Specify corner of window, enter a scale factor or [nX/nXP}, or
[All/Center/Dynamic/Extents/Previous/Scale/Window] <real time>: *pick* **a corner for**
window
>>>Specify opposite corner: *pick*
Resuming ELLIPSE command.

63

Assignments

1. Construct the hexagon using the **Polygon** tool (top left-hand drawing). Add its diagonals using the **Line** tool. **Erase** the pentagon (central top drawing).

   ▪ Construct the pentagon (bottom left-hand drawing). Add its diagonals. Erase the pentagon (central bottom drawing).

   ▪ Construct both the top right-hand and bottom right-hand drawings using the **Polygon** tool. It will be necessary to use osnaps to produce accurate drawings.

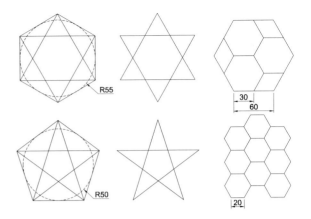

2. Construct the given drawing using the **Polyline**, **Ellipse**, **Rectangle** and **Polygon** tools.

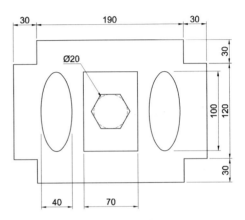

3. Using the **Polygon** and **Ellipse** tools, construct the given drawing. Use osnaps to ensure accurate positioning of the ellipses.

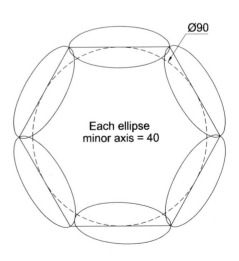

Each ellipse minor axis = 40

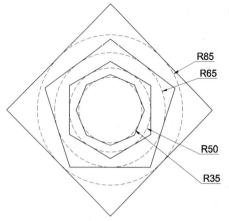

4. Construct the polygons as shown.

R85
R65
R50
R35

5. Construct the given drawing using the **Polyline**, **Ellipse** and **Rectangle** tools.

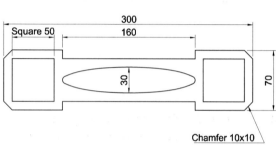

300
Square 50 160
30
70
Chamfer 10x10

The Trim tool

To call the **Trim** *left-click* on its icon in the **Modify** toolbar, or on its name in the **Modify** drop-down menu, or *enter* **tr** or **trim** at the command line.

Trim

First example – trim: Edge=None (left-hand drawings)

Command: _trim
Current settings: Projection=UCS, Edge=None
Select cutting edges ...
Select objects: *pick* **1 found**
Select objects: *pick* **2 total**
Select objects: *right-click*
Select object to trim or shift-select to extend or [Project/Edge/Undo]: *pick*
Select object to trim or shift-select to extend or [Project/Edge/Undo]: *pick*
Select object to trim or shift-select to extend or [Project/Edge/Undo]: *right-click*
Command:

Second example – trim: Edge=Extend (right-hand drawings)

At the prompt line:

Select object to trim or shift-select to extend or [Project/Edge/Undo]: *enter* **e** *right-click*
Enter an implied edge extension mode [Extend/No extend]: *enter* **e** *right-click*
Then when **Trim** is called, the first prompt line becomes:

Current settings: Projection=UCS, Edge=Extend

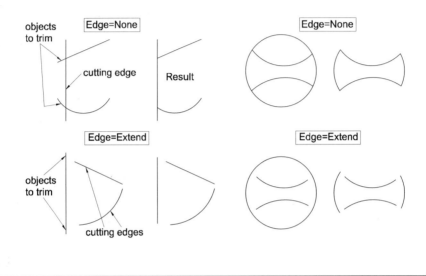

The Array tool

To call the **Array** tool *left-click* on its icon in the
Modify toolbar, or on its name in the **Modify**
drop-down menu, or *enter* **ar** or **array** at the
command line.

Notes

Arrays can be **Rectangular (R)** or **Polar (P)**.

First example – a Rectangular Array

1. Construct the chamfered rectangle around a circle – top left-hand part of the drawing.

2. Call the **Array** tool. The **Array** dialog appears.

3. In the dialog *enter* figures as shown:

   ■ **Rows:** 6

   ■ **Columns:** 10

   ■ **Row Offset:** -40

   ■ **Column Offset:** 40

   Note the distance between rows may well be a negative number. This is because the distance between rows is measured along the **Y** coordinate axis.

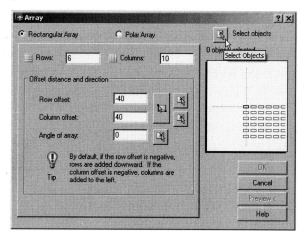

4. *Left-click* the **Select Objects** button.

5. The dialog disappears. Select the rectangle and circle previously constructed. The dialog reappears.

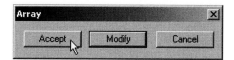

6. *Left-click* the **Preview** button of the dialog. The dialog disappears and the drawing appears on screen with the array showing, together with a warning box.

7. If the array is as wished, *left-click* the **Accept** button. If the array is to be changed *left-click* the **Modify** button and make necessary changes in the **Array** dialog.

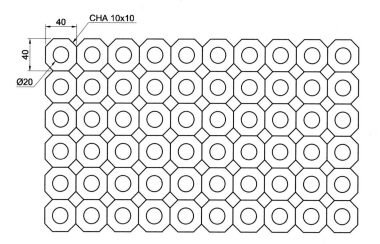

Second example – a Polar Array

1. Construct the given circle and the head of a bolt held in position by a nut at the top of the top of the circle – top right-hand drawing shows a scaled-up version of this drawing.

2. Call the **Array** tool and make *entries* in the **Array** dialog as shown.

3. *Left-click* the **Select Objects** button and window the nut and its bolt. The dialog box reappears.

4. *Left-click* the **Pick Center Point** button. The dialog disappears, the drawing reappears with the warning box centrally placed.

5. If satisfied with the array, *left-click* the **Accept** button.

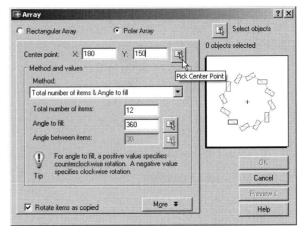

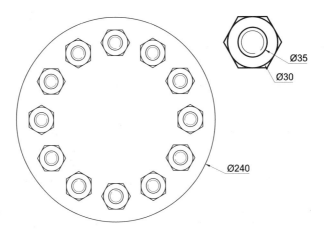

Third example – a Polar Array

1. Construct the arrow using the **Polyline** tool.

2. Call the **Array** tool. The **Array** dialog appears.

3. Make the necessary *entries* in the dialog as shown. Note the **Angle to fill:** is -180. This is because the default rotation in AutoCAD is counter-clockwise.

4. *Left-click* the **Select Objects** button and select the arrow.

5. *Left-click* the **Pick Center Point** button and *pick* the central point around which the arrow is to array.

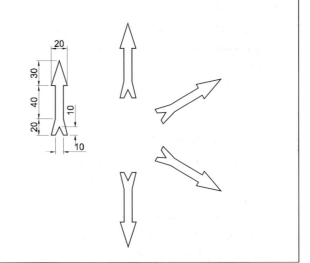

The Offset tool

To call the **Offset** tool *left-click* on its icon in the **Modify** toolbar, or on its name in the **Modify** drop-down menu, or *enter* **o** or **offset** at the command line.

When the tool is called the command line shows:

Command:_offset
Specify offset distance or [Through]:
enter **15** *right-click*
Select object to offset <exit>: *pick*
Specify point on side to offset: *pick*

OR

Command:_offset
Specify offset distance or [Through]: *pick*
2 points (the distance apart required for the offset)
Select object to offset <exit>: *pick*
Specify point on side to offset: *pick*

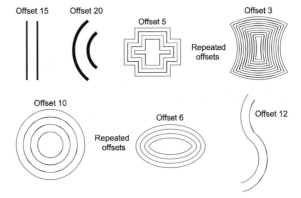

Assignments

1. Working to the given dimensions, construct the
left-hand drawing. With the **TRIM** tool
produce the end view as shown. Then add the
front view.

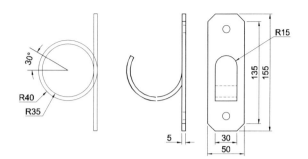

2. Using the tools, **Ellipse**, **Circle**, **Offset**,
and **Array** construct the given drawing.
The larger ellipses are arrayed 12 times
and the smaller 30 times.

3. With the tools **Circle**, **Trim**, **Polyline**
and **Edit Polyline** construct the view
of a file handle as shown, working to
the given dimensions.

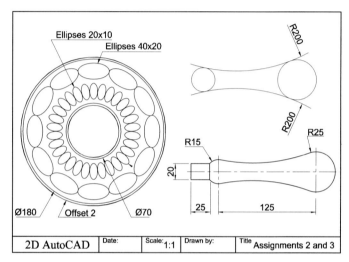

2D AutoCAD	Date:	Scale: 1:1	Drawn by:	Title Assignments 2 and 3

4. Construct the left-hand drawing using the
Polyline and **Offset** tools. Then using the
Trim tool complete the right-hand drawing.

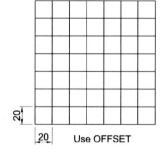

Use OFFSET

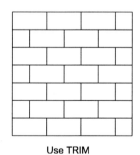

Use TRIM

5. Using the **Polyline** tool set to a width of **1**, construct the left-hand drawing to the given dimensions. Then from the drawing and using the **Trim** tool complete the exercise to produce the right-hand drawing.

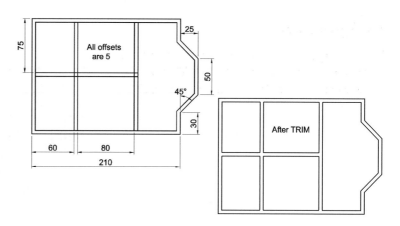

6. Construct the drawing labelled **Stage 2** as shown and from that drawing produce the array as given in the right-hand drawing.

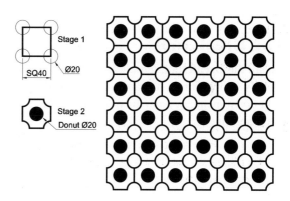

7. Construct the array working to the instructions given with the drawing.

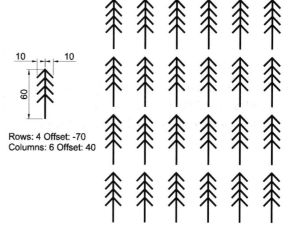

Rows: 4 Offset: -70
Columns: 6 Offset: 40

71

8. Construct this array working to the same instructions as in exercise 9 above, but with the **Angle of array** set at **300**.

The Break tool

To call the **Break** tool, *left-click* on its icon in the **Modify** toolbar, or on its name in the **Modify** drop-down menu, or *enter* **br** or **break** at the command line.

Break

First example – a line, an arc and a circle

1. Open the template **A3_template.dwt**.

2. Construct a line, an arc and a circle to any dimensions.

3. Call the **Break** tool.

4. Using **Break** on every one of the three objects in turn.

Command:_break Select object: *pick*
Specify second break point or
[First point]: *pick*
Command:

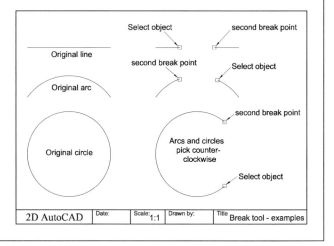

Second example – using the First option

1. Draw a line of any length.

2. Call the Break tool:

Command:_break Select object: *pick*
Specify second break point or [First point]:
enter f right-click
Specify first break point: *pick*
Specify second break point: *pick*
Command:

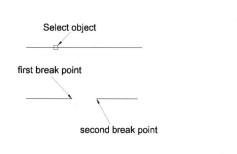

Select object

first break point

second break point

The Scale tool

To call the **Scale** tool *left-click* on its icon in the **Modify** toolbar or on its name in the **Modify** drop-down menu, or *enter* **sc** or **scale** at the command line.

Examples

1. Open the **A3_template.dwt** template.

2. Construct drawing 1. using **Rectangle** with **Fillet** R20. With **Pedit** makes its **Width**=2. Add the circles and rectangle using the **Polyline** tool.

3. Multiple Copy the drawing 4 times.

4. Call the **Scale** tool:

Command: _scale
Select objects: window first copy
Specify opposite corner: 6 found
Select objects: *right-click*
Specify Base point: *pick*
Specify scale factor or [Reference]:
enter **0.5** *right-click*
Command:

Repeat for the other three copies scaling to the figures shown in the drawings.

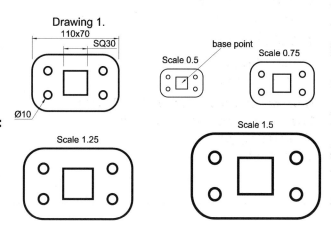

Drawing 1.
110x70
SQ30
Ø10

base point
Scale 0.5
Scale 0.75
Scale 1.25
Scale 1.5

The Extend tool

To call the **Extend** tool, *left-click* on its icon in the **Modify** toolbar, or on its name in the **Modify** drop-down menu, or *enter* **ex** or **extend** at the command line.

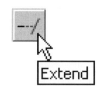

First example – Extend

1. **Open A3_template.dwt** template.

2. There are four examples. Construct each of the preliminary drawings to any suitable sizes.

3. Call the **Extend** tool:

Command:_extend
Current settings: Projection=None, Edge= None
Select boundary edges ...
Select objects: *pick* **1 found**
Select objects: *right-click*
Select object to extend or shift-select to trim or [Project/Edge/Undo]: *pick*
Select object to extend or shift-select to trim or [Project/Edge/Undo]: *pick*
Select object to extend or shift-select to trim or [Project/Edge/Undo]: *right-click*
Command:

Second example – the Extend option

At the prompt line:

Select object to extend or shift-select to trim or [Project/Edge/Undo]: *enter* **e** *right-click*
Enter an implied edge extension mode [Extend/No extend] <No extend>: *enter* **e** *right-click*

An implied extension can be made as shown in the two right-hand examples.

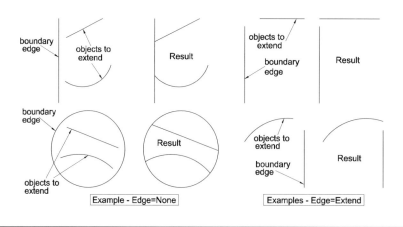

Two worked examples using Modify tools

First example

1. **Open** the **A3_template.dwt** template.

2. To construct the example:

(a) **Drawing 1**. Construct the circles and polyline as shown.

(b) **Drawing 2**. Using **Trim**, trim the polyline back to the Ø200 circle and the Ø30 circle to a semicircle.

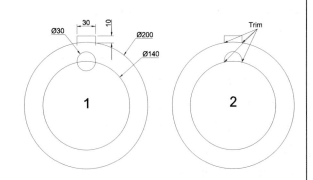

(c) **Drawing 3**. Using **Array**, polar array the polyline 12 times around the Ø200 circle.

With **Rotate**, rotate the part circle by 60°.

With **Mirror**, mirror the semicircle horizontally, then mirror the two semicircles vertically.

(d) **Drawing 4.** With **Trim**, trim away parts of the circles no longer required.

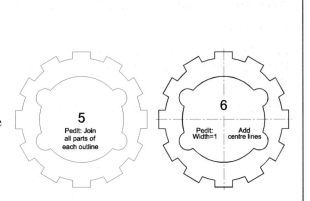

(e) **Drawing 5.** With **Pedit**, join the two parts of the drawing into single polylines.

(f) **Drawing 6.** With **Pedit** change the line width to 1.

Make layer **Centre** current layer and add centre lines

Second example

1. **Open** the **A3_template.dwt** template.

2. To construct the example:

   (a) **Drawing 1.** Construct the drawing as shown. Use **Osnap int** to ensure the Ø15 circles are accurately positioned.

   (b) **Drawings 2 and 3.** With **Trim** trim the circles as shown. With **Pedit** join the arcs.

   (c) **Drawing 3.** With **Array**, array the closed arcs 6 times around the centre of the Ø170 circle. Add the Ø50 circle.

   With **Pedit** change the line widths throughout the drawing to 0.7. This involves the use of the **Break** tool when changing the line widths of the circles.

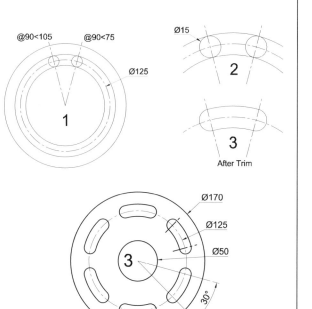

The Chamfer tool

To call **Chamfer** *left-click* on its icon in the **Modify** toolbar, or on its name in the **Modify** drop-down menu, or by *entering* **cha** or **chamfer** at the command line.

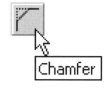

First example – Chamfer (Trim mode)

1. **Open** the **A3_template.dwt** template.

2. Construct a rectangle (any dimensions) with the **Line** tool.

3. Call **Chamfer**:

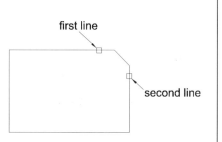

Command:_chamfer
(TRIM mode) Current chamfer distance Dist1=1, Dist2=1
Select first line or [Polyline/Distance/Angle/Trim/Method]: *enter* d (Distance) *right-click*
Specify first chamfer distance <1>: *enter* 15 *right-click*
Specify second chamfer distance <15>: *right-click*
Select first line or [Polyline/Distance/Angle/Trim/Method]: *pick*
Select second line or [Polyline/Distance/Angle/Trim/Method]: *pick*
Command:

Second example – Chamfer (No trim mode)

To set the prompts to the **No Trim** mode:

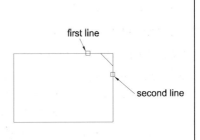

first line

second line

Command:_chamfer
(TRIM mode) Current chamfer distance Dist1=1, Dist2=1
Select first line or
[Polyline/Distance/Angle/Trim/Method]: *enter* **t (Trim)**
right-click
Enter Trim mode option [Trim/No Trim] <Trim>: *enter* **n**
(No Trim) *right-click*

Now proceed as in the first example.

Third example – Chamfer (Polyline – Trim mode)

1. Construct a **Polyline** rectangle (any dimensions) of **Width=1.5**.

2. Call the **Chamfer** tool:

3. Set the prompts to **Trim mode**.

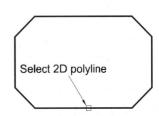

Select 2D polyline

Command:_chamfer
(TRIM mode) Current chamfer distance Dist1=1, Dist2=1
Select first line or [Polyline/Distance/Angle/Trim/Method]:
enter **d (Distance)** *right-click*
Specify first chamfer distance <1>: *enter* **20** *right-click*
Specify second chamfer distance <20>: *right-click*
Select first line or [Polyline/Distance/Angle/Trim/Method]:
enter **p** *right-click*
Select 2D polyline: *pick* the pline
Command:

Fourth example – Chamfer (Polyline – Trim mode)

1. Construct a **Polyline** similar to that shown in
    the drawing **1** to a **Width=2**.

2. Call the **Chamfer** tool, set **Dist1** and **Dist2 to
    10**, use the **Polyline** option and select the
    drawing. The result is shown in drawing **2**.

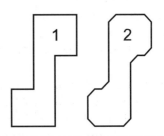

Notes

1. If a chamfer is constructed with **Dist1** different to **Dist2**, the chamfer will be sloping at an angle other than 45°.

2. A similar result (a chamfer at an angle other than 45°) can be obtained by making use of the **Angle** option in response to the prompts line. As an example:

   Command:_chamfer
   Select first line or [Polyline/Distance/Angle/Trim/Method]: *enter* **a** *right-click*
   Specify chamfer length on first line <1>: *enter* **15** *right-click*
   Specify chamfer angle from the first line <0>: *enter* **30** *right-click*
   Select first line or [Polyline/Distance/Angle/Trim/Method]: *pick*
   Select second line: *pick*

3. The four examples of chamfer could all have been constructed in a single window in an **A3_layout.dwt** as shown below.

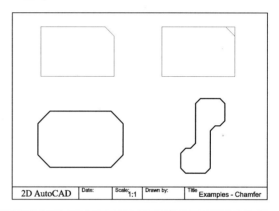

2D AutoCAD	Date:	Scale: 1:1	Drawn by:	Title Examples - Chamfer

The Fillet tool

Fillet can be called from the **Modify** toolbar, from the **Modify** drop-down menu, by *entering* f at the Command line.

Fillet

First example

1. **Open** the **A3_template.dwt** template.

2. Construct three rectangles (any dimensions) with the **Line** tool and the outline given in the bottom right-hand drawing (again any sizes).

3. Call **Fillet**.

Prompts for **Fillet** are much the same as for **Chamfer** The only real difference is that instead of settings figures for distances (**Dist1** and **Dist2**) figures for **Radius** are *entered* instead.

The examples shown above and below were constructed using similar responses as for those for the **Chamfer** examples.

Second example – fillets between lines and circles

Fillets between circles or arcs, between circles and lines or between arcs can be constructed using the **Fillet** tool. Three examples are given: left-hand trio of drawings between circles and a line; centre pair of drawings between circles; the right-hand trio between a line and an arc.

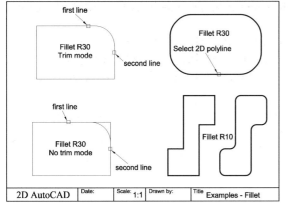

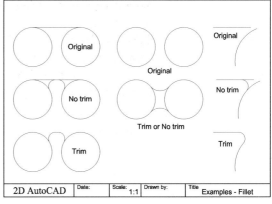

Hatching

To call the **Hatch** tool, *left-click* on the **Hatch** icon in the **Draw** toolbar or on **Hatch...** in the **Draw** drop-down menu, or *enter* h at the command line. Note that **hatch** *entered* at the command line does not produce the same result. No matter which of these methods is used to call Hatch the **Boundary Hatch and Fill** dialog appears on screen.

A *left-click* on the **Advanced** tab brings another dialog on screen from which the **Advanced** options can be selected if wished.

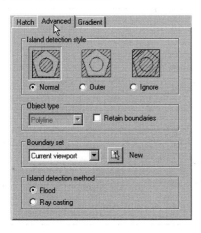

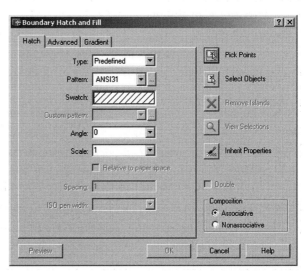

A *left-click* in the **Swatch** field of the **Boundary Hatch and Fill** dialog brings the first of the **Hatch Pattern Palette** dialogs on screen (the **ANSI** palette).

There are three other **Hatch Pattern Palette** dialogs. The **Other Predefined** dialog is also shown. As will be shown later the **Hatch Pattern Palette** dialogs allow a variety of hatch patterns to be selected when hatching drawings.

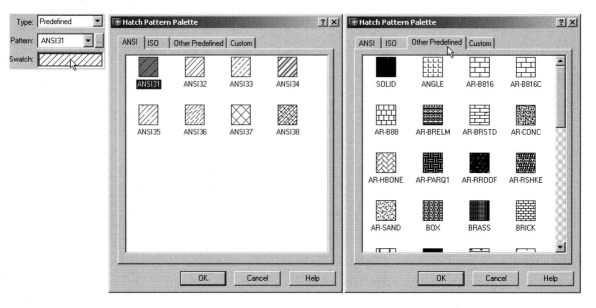

Examples of hatching areas of drawings

First example

1. **Open** the **A4_template.dwt** template.

2. Construct the chamfered rectangle shown in the upper drawing. Call **Hatch**.

3. In the **Boundary Hatch and Fill** dialog *left-click* in the **Swatch** field and select the pattern **ANSI1** from the **Hatch Pattern Palette**. Then *left-click* the **Pick Points** button of the dialog.

4. The dialog disappears. *Left-click* in the rectangle which has been constructed.

5. The dialog reappears. *Left-click* the **Preview** button of the dialog. If the preview in the rectangle is as wished, *left-click* the **OK** button of the dialog.

6. If not, *right-click* and amend the settings in the dialog which reappears with the *right-click* and follow the same procedure again.

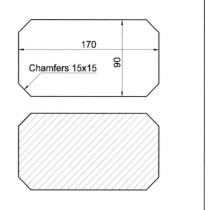

Second example – Advanced options

1. **Open** the **A4_template.dwt** template.

2. Construct the top left-hand drawing.

3. **Multiple Copy** the drawing three times.

4. *Left-click* on the **Normal** radio button in the **Advanced** dialog, followed by a *left-click* on the **Select Objects** button. Then window the top-right copy.

5. Repeat using the **Outer** option button on the bottom left-hand copy.

6. Finally repeat using the **Ignore** option button on the bottom right-hand copy.

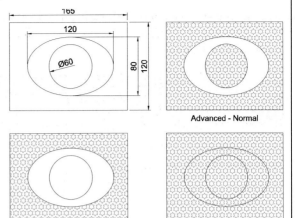

Advanced - Normal

Advanced - Outer

Advanced - Ignore

Third example – Associative hatch option

1. **Open** the **A4_template.dwt** template.

2. Construct the left-hand drawing.

3. In the **Hatch Boundary** dialog, make sure the **Associative** radio button is set on (dot in circle). See bottom right-hand corner of the **Hatch Boundary** dialog.

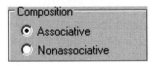

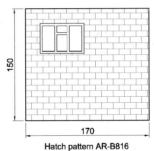

Hatch pattern AR-B816
Scale 1

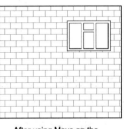

After using Move on the
window framework

4. Using the **Advanced Outer** option hatch the drawing using the **AR-B816** hatch pattern set to **Scale=1** from the **Other Defined Hatch Pattern** palette.

5. Using the **Move** tool with a window option move the window framework to the right as shown in the right-hand drawing. The hatch pattern accommodates to the move – it is "associative".

Fourth example – section in an engineering technical drawing

Sectional views are important in technical drawings – they show the shapes of parts which cannot be seen in an outside view. The object is imagined as having been cut by a cutting plane and the part behind the cutting plane removed so showing the cut surfaces.

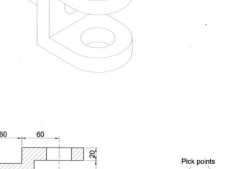

A pictorial drawing of fork coupling is shown. To construct a two-view orthographic projection of the coupling to include a sectional view:

1. **Open** the **A4_template.dwt** template.

2. Construct the two views as shown without the hatching. Do not include the dimensions.

3. Call the **Hatch** tool. Set the hatch pattern to **ANSI31** with a **Scale = 40**.

4. *Left-click* on the **Pick Points** – *pick* points as shown in the right-hand drawing – copy of the outline of the front view.

5. Note the section plane line labelled with **A** each end and the label **A-A** with the sectional view.

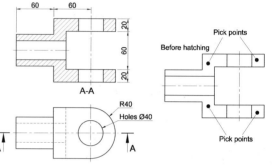

Fifth example – section in an engineering technical drawing

As a general rule parts such as webs, pins, rods, spindles and other cylindrical parts are shown by outside views within sections. A two-view projection including a sectional view is shown below.

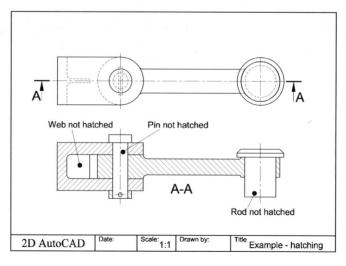

1. The **Preview** button in the **Boundary Hatch and Fill** dialog may need a *double-click* to bring a preview on screen.

2. When selecting an area to be hatched, it **MUST** be a closed boundary. If an area is *picked* which is not closed – even with the slightest gap in the outline – the **Boundary Definition Error** warning box will appear. This does not necessarily mean the area cannot be hatched. Try the **Select Objects** button instead and *pick* each object forming the boundary of the area to be hatched.

3. If the **Boundary Definition Error** warning box does appear, it is however advisable to check where the boundary is not closed.

Dimensions

AutoCAD has a large variety of methods for dimensioning drawings. It is advisable to experiment with the variety of methods in order to be able to take full advantage of the methods available in AutoCAD.

Both the **A3_template.dwt** and the **A4_template.dwt** templates include a style of dimensioning already set up from the **Dimension Style** dialog (page 32).

The Dimension toolbar

To call the toolbar to the screen *right-click* in any toolbar, followed by a *left-click* on the name **Dimension** in the menu which appears. In the illustration below, the **Linear Dimension** tool from the toolbar has been *picked*.

Example – dimlinear

1. **Open** the **A3_template.dwt** template and construct the outline shown using the polyline tool.

2. *Left-click* the **Linear Dimension** tool icon.

Command:_dimlinear
Specify first extension line origin: *pick*
Specify second dimension line origin: *pick*
Specify dimension line location: *pick*
Dimension text = 120
Command: *right-click*
Command:_dimlinear
Specify first extension line origin: *pick*
Specify second dimension line origin: *pick*
Specify dimension line location: *pick*
Dimension text = 70
Command:

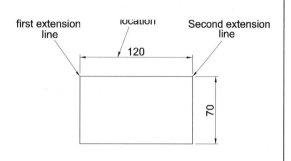

The Multiple Document Environment (MDE)

Several drawings can be opened into the AutoCAD window allowing parts of drawings to be moved or copied from drawing to drawing if required.

Example – MDE

1. Open four drawings from those saved from constructing the examples or assignments. They can be opened one after the other because a large number of drawings can be opened in AutoCAD at the same time. In the example given, four drawings from this book have been opened.

2. *Left-click* on **Window** in the menu bar and in the drop-down menu *left-click* on **Tile Horizontally**.

3. The four drawings appear in the window.

4. *Left-click* in each window in turn and call **Zoom** by *entering* **z** at the command line and *entering* **e** (for **Extents**) in answer to the prompts which then appear. The four drawings appear as shown.

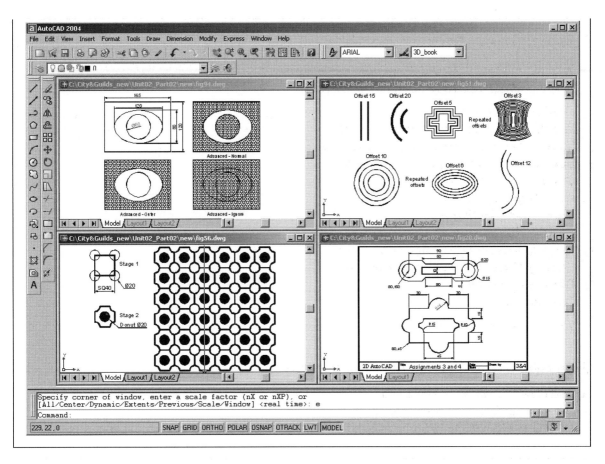

Assignments

1. Use the **Polyline** and **Rectangle** tools to construct the left-hand drawing. With **Pedit** change the line width to **1**. Then with the **Chamfer** tool chamfer the various corners as shown in the right-hand drawing.

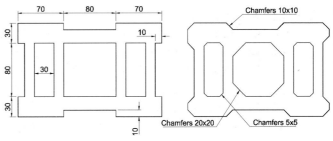

2. **Construct** a straight line outline using the **Polyline** tool (**Width=1**) to the dimensions as given. Then using the **Chamfer** and **Fillet** tools, chamfer and fillet the corners of your outline as shown.

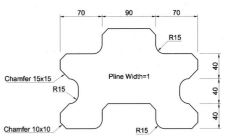

3. Using the **Line** and **Circle** tools construct the upper drawing to the given dimensions. Then using the **Trim** and **Fillet** tools produce the lower drawing. When completed change the line widths of all parts of your drawing using the **Pedit** tool.

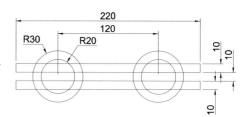

All fillets are R5

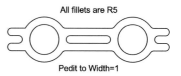

Pedit to Width=1

4. A simple bracket is shown in a pictorial drawing. A three-view orthographic projection is also given. Copy the orthographic projection working to the given dimensions.

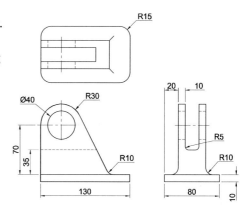

5. Working to the dimensions given, construct these two drawings.

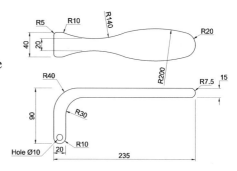

6. Make an accurate copy of the pulley as shown, working to the sizes as given.

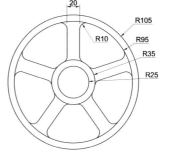

7. Construct the drawing **1** using the **Line** and **Arc** tools. Using the **Fillet** tool amend your drawing to produce the drawing **2**. Further amend your drawing using the **Edit Polyline** tool to change the lien width to **1**. Add the **Pline** circles.

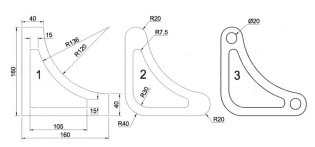

8. Construct four rectangles as shown (120×70) using a pline of width = 1. Amend each corner as shown to a dimension of 15. Then hatch each rectangle as indicated.

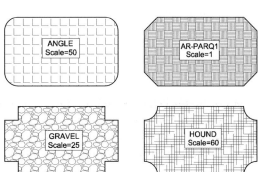

9. Using **Polyline** (**Width=1**) construct a rectangle 305×95. Fillet its corner to a radius of 20. Offset the rectangle by 10. Then:

Command: *enter* **dt** *right-click*
Current text style: "ARIAL" Text height: 8
Specify start point of text: *pick*
Specify rotation angle of text <0>: *right-click*
Enter text: *enter* **AutoCAD** *right-click*
Command:

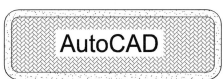

Then **Scale** the text by **3** and add appropriate hatching.

10. Construct the given end view of a house. Add the hatching as indicated. Then with **Move** move the window to a different position noting the action of **Associative hatching**.

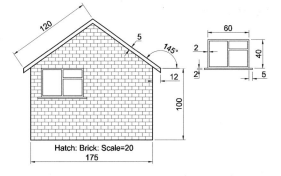

11. Construct the crossing ellipses and circle pattern. Hatch the pattern. With **Array** construct the rectangular array as shown. Add the surrounding rectangle using **Polyline** to **Width=1**. **Offset** the rectangle by **10** and hatch the area the offset rectangles contains.

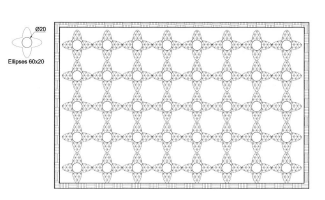

12. A pictorial drawing of a bracket with a rod is shown together with a three-view orthographic projection of the bracket which includes a sectional view. Construct the three-view projection. Do not include any of the dimensions.

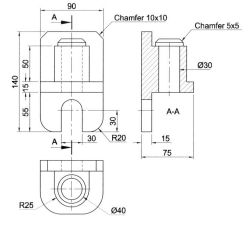

13. A front view of a house is shown. The view incorporates several hatched areas. Working to the given dimensions hatch the various parts of the drawing as shown. Do not include any of the dimensions.

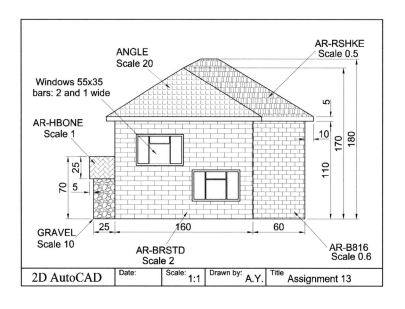

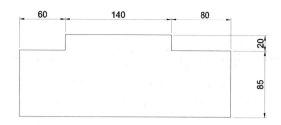

14. Using the **Line** tool, construct the outline shown. Then add the dimensions using the **Linear Dimension** tool from the **Dimension** toolbar.

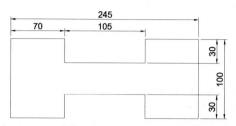

15. Using the **Line** tool, construct the outline shown. Then add the dimensions using the **Linear Dimension** tool from the **Dimension** toolbar.

Theory of 2D CAD

Here are 100 questions designed for testing what has been learned from Chapters 1, 2 and 3. In the following series of questions, the multi-part questions mostly have a single answer, but where it is thought there is more than one answer make sure all are named.

1. There are two methods described earlier for loading AutoCAD ready for use. Can you name them?

2. When AutoCAD has been loaded three buttons appear at the top right-hand corner of the screen. To close AutoCAD a *left-click* on which button is needed?

  (a) The button with a hyphen (-).

  (b) The button with a square icon.

  (c) The button with a cross.

3. Which toolbars usually appear on the left-hand side in the AutoCAD window when the software is loaded?

  (a) The **Modify** toolbar.

  (b) The **View** toolbar.

  (c) The **Draw** toolbar.

  (d) The **Object Snap** toolbar.

4. Two other toolbars usually appear at the top of the AutoCAD window when it is loaded. Can you name them?

5. To *double-click* mouse buttons when working in AutoCAD means:

  (a) press both buttons of the mouse at the same time;

  (b) press the right-hand button twice;

  (c) press the left-hand button twice;

  (d) press both buttons at the same time twice.

6. What is a **flyout**?

7. Why is it important to make backup files when constructing drawings in AutoCAD?

  (a) Because it is good practise to have two copies of a drawing.

  (b) In case a computer failure causes the loss of a drawing.

  (c) In order to save disk space.

  (d) To avoid a drawing being saved to the wrong name.

8. A popup list will appear:

  (a) with a *left-click* on the query (**?**) button which appears at the top right-hand corner of some dialogs;

  (b) with a *left-click* on the arrow which appears at the side of some information fields;

  (c) with a *right-click* anywhere in the AutoCAD window;

  (d) when a *double-click* is made in a toolbar.

9. What is meant by **Associative Help**?

10. What happens if the **F1** key of the keyboard is pressed when a tool is in action when working in AutoCAD?

11. Which of the following menus can be selected from the menu bar?

    (a) right-click.

    (b) drop-down.

    (c) left-click.

    (d) the toolbars menu.

12. Which is the filename extension for an AutoCAD drawing?

    (a) dwt.

    (b) bak.

    (c) dwg.

    (d) draw.

13. What is a sub-directory?

14. Why is it important to back-up files as they are constructed?

15. A "byte" is:

    (a) 16 bits;

    (b) 8 bits;

    (c) the same as a kilobyte;

    (d) a single bit.

16. A Hertz is a cycle per second. What is a Gigahertz?

17. When a computer is said to be running at 2 Gigahertz at which speed is it running?

    (a) 200,000 Hertz;

    (b) 2000,000,000 Hertz

    (c) 2,000,000,000 Hertz;

    (d) 20,000 Hertz.

18. What is a VDU?

19. Can hard disks be removed from a computer?

20. Which of the following are peripherals?

    (a) A hard disk.

    (b) A printer.

    (c) The monitor screen.

    (d) A mouse.

    (e) A keyboard.

    (f) A scanner.

    (g) Windows.

21. When using a computer:

    (a) is it advisable to eat one's lunch at the same time?

    (b) is it advisable to drink a cup of tea?

    (c) should one take breaks at regular intervals of time?

    (d) should one use a document holder?

22. What do the initials www stand for?

23. When constructing a drawing in AutoCAD, snap allows the operator to:

    (a) use the mouse more easily;

    (b) see at which coordinate point the cursors are positioned;

    (c) to see a set of grid points on the screen.

    (d) to move the cursor under mouse control between set points.

24. What is the difference between relative coordinate entry and absolute coordinate entry when drawing in AutoCAD?

25. What is meant by the AutoCAD coordinate system?

26. Which is the default rotational direction for the sizes of angles to be read in AutoCAD?

    (a) Counter-clockwise.

    (b) Clockwise.

    (c) Depends on which way the operator wishes to work.

    (d) Depends upon the angle being measured.

27. Why use osnaps?

28. When using osnaps how can the size of the *pick* box be altered?

 (a) By *picking* a corner of the box and *dragging* to the required size.

 (b) In the **Drafting Settings** dialog.

 (c) In the **Options** dialog.

 (d) It cannot be altered.

29. The **Line** tool can be called by?

 (a) *Entering* **l** at the command line.

 (b) *Entering* **lin** at the command line.

 (c) With a *left-click* on the **Line** tool icon in the **Draw** toolbar.

 (d) Selecting **Line** from the **Draw** drop-down menu.

30. The advantage of using the **Polyline** tool is?

 (a) It is quicker to use than the **Line** tool.

 (b) Lines of varying widths can be drawn.

 (c) All lines in a polyline outline form a single object.

 (d) Arcs can be drawn using the tool.

31. What is the difference between drawing an outline using absolute unit entry compared with using relative coordinate entry?

32. When using the **Erase** tool a crossing window:

 (a) erases only objects inside the window;

 (b) erases all objects crossed by the lines of the window;

 (c) does not erase any objects in the drawing;

 (d) a crossing window cannot be used with the **Erase** tool.

33. What happens when the following function keys are pressed?

 (a) **F7**

 (b) **F8**

 (c) **F9**

 (d) **F6**

34. How is a circle constructed with the aid of the **Polyline** tool?

35. To what **Limits** should a template for an A3 drawing sheet be set?

 (a) 297,210;

 (b) 420,297;

 (c) 594,420;

 (d) 210,149.

36. What is the purpose of setting **Snap** to **5**?

 (a) To allow the cursor under mouse control to only move in steps of 5 units in all directions.

 (b) To allow for greater accuracy when constructing outlines.

 (c) To snap to grid points.

 (d) To allow only vertical and/or horizontal lines to be drawn.

37. How can the text font **Romand.shx** be renamed **My-text**?

38. What is the purpose of saving an AutoCAD windows setup as a template file?

39. What is the file extension for an AutoCAD drawing template?

 (a) *.dwg;

 (b) *.dwt;

 (c) *.dxf;

 (d) *.dwt.

40. The linetype scale is set to **30** for the **A3** drawing template, but to **15** for the **A4** template. Can you explain why this is so?

41. Certain keyboard keys can be used for changing the coordinates shown in the status bar from showing absolute coordinates to relative coordinates or to no coordinates. These two keys are?

(a) Ctrl+V

(b) Ctrl+D

(c) Ctrl+C

(d) Ctrl+Z.

42. What is the difference between a **realtime** zoom and a **Window** zoom?

43. When working with a very large drawing how does an operator move from one part of a drawing to another?

(a) By making use of the **Pan** tool.

(b) By using the **Zoom** tool and the **Window** prompt.

(c) By using a combination of the **Window** prompt of the **Zoom** tool, together with the **Pan** tool.

(d) By scrolling the AutoCAD window from the scroll bars.

44. What is a toolbar?

(a) It is a menu in which tool icons are held.

(b) It is a dialog in which tool icons are shown.

(c) It is a specific part of AutoCAD in which tools icons of a group of commands is shown.

(d) It is a bar at the bottom of the AutoCAD window.

45. There are two methods of placing text in a drawing. Can you name them? Also which of the following is the abbreviation for one type of text?

(a) te

(b) dt

(c) text

(d) st

46. Can text be added to an AutoCAD drawing in **bold** style? Which of the styles of text font might be so *entered*?

(a) AutoCAD fonts.

(b) Windows True Type fonts.

(c) Any text style.

(d) It is not possible.

47. Can you write down the stages needed to change the style of text font in use from **ROMAND** to **Times New Roman**?

48. Have you experimented with the **Symbols** popup list from the **Multiline Text Editor** dialog?

49. When checking spelling which of the following can be used?

(a) The **Spelling** tool.

(b) By setting parameters in the **Text Style** dialog.

(c) *Entering* **ddedit** at the command line and following prompts at the command line.

(d) By settings in the **Options** dialog.

50. What is the difference between using the **dtext** tool and the **Mtext** tool?

51. How is the **Aerial View** window brought into the AutoCAD window?

52. **AutoSnap** will only function if:

(a) osnaps are off;

(b) osnaps are on;

(c) snap is set to 5 units;

(d) grid is set on.

53. From which dialog can **AutoSnap** be setup?

54. What is an **AutoSnap** tip?

55. The outline of a circle drawn using the **Circle** tool can be made wider by:

(a) using the **pedit** tool;

(b) using the **Break** tool followed by using the **pedit** tool;

(c) it is not possible;

(d) using one of the prompts which appear at the command line when **Circle** is called.

56. Which prompt of the **Circle** options is used for drawing a circle tangential to two lines at right angles to each other?

(a) The **3P** prompt.

(b) The **2P** prompt.

(c) The **ttr** prompt.

(d) The **first tangent** prompt.

57. Can an arc be constructed using the **Polyline** tool and if so how?

58. Which of the following abbreviations can be *entered* at the command line when calling the **Break** tool?

(a) b

(b) brea

(c) br

(d) There is no abbreviation for the tool.

59. What is the abbreviation for the **Polyline Edit** tool?

60. In which direction do breaks occur when using **Break** on an arc?

(a) Counter-clockwise.

(b) Clockwise.

(c) Any direction.

(d) The tool cannot be used to break an arc.

61. Can you name the abbreviations for the commonly used osnap tools?

62. What is the purpose of using the set variable **PELLIPSE**?

(a) To allow ellipses to be drawn.

(b) When set to **1**, ellipses are polyline ellipses.

(c) Allows both axes to be of set sizes.

(d) When set to **2**, allows true ellipses to be drawn.

63. What is the difference between a regular and an irregular polygon?

(a) The sides of a regular polygon are all of equal length.

(b) The angles of a regular polygon are not all of equal size.

(c) The angles of a regular polygon are all of equal size.

(d) The sides and angles of an irregular polygon are of unequal lengths and sizes.

64. What are the names of the two axes of an ellipse?

65. How can the width of the lines of a polygon be changed?

66. What is the purpose of the **Elevation** option in the sequence of prompts seen when the **Rectangle** tool is called?

67. What is the command line abbreviation for the tool **Circle**?

(a) ci

(b) c

(c) cc

(d) cir.

68. What is the command line abbreviation for the tool **Move**?

(a) mov

(b) mo

(c) m

(d) mm

69. What is the command line abbreviation for the **Array** tool?

   (a) arr

   (b) ar

   (c) a

   (d) ay.

70. The **Array** tool can be used for constructing two types of array. What are these two types?

71. What is an array?

72. What is the difference between using the **No extend** and **Extend** options within the **Trim** prompts sequence?

73. What is the command line abbreviation for the tool **Offset**?

   (a) o

   (b) of

   (c) off

   (d) ofs.

74. Can the **Offset** tool be used to construct a similar drawing to the **Array** tool?

75. Can you explain the differences between **AutoSnap** and **Object Snap**?

76. When would you use the **F** option of the **Break** tool?

   (a) When you wish to finish using the tool.

   (b) When you wish to break an object at two selected points.

   (c) To select the first of 2 points when breaking an object.

   (d) When you have made a mistake and wish to use another prompt of the tool.

77. What is the default direction of angles when using AutoCAD?

   (a) Anticlockwise.

   (b) Clockwise.

   (c) In any direction.

   (d) There is no default direction.

78. How does this affect the use of the **Break** tool when using the tool on a circle?

79. What are the differences between using the **Extend** and the **No extend** options of the **Extend** tool?

80. Is it possible to fillet one corner of a polyline rectangle?

81. Is it possible to use the **Fillet** tool to form a sharp corner from two lines which do not meet at the corner?

   (a) Yes – by setting **Radius** to **0**.

   (b) No – it is not possible.

   (c) Yes – but only if the if the lines are made to meet by using the **Extend** tool.

82. What is the abbreviation for the **Chamfer** tool?

   (a) cha

   (b) ch

   (c) cham

   (d) There is no abbreviation. **Chamfer** must be *entered* in full.

83. What is the abbreviation for the **Fillet** tool?

84. Can a fillet be formed between two adjacent circles?

85. What is the abbreviation for the **Hatch** tool?

86. Have you tried *entering* **hatch** at the command line rather than **h**? Try doing so and see what happens.

87. What is **Associative hatching**?

   (a) Hatching which associates two hatch patterns.

   (b) Hatching associated with the boundary being hatched.

   (c) Hatching which accommodates to changes made to areas within the hatched area.

   (d) Hatching associated with other hatched areas within a drawing.

88. Why is **Associative hatching** important under some circumstances?

89. There are two methods of selecting an area to be hatched. Can you describe them?

90. What is usually wrong if the **Boundary Definition Error** warning appears when a preview is requested?

    (a) The area cannot be hatched.

    (b) The boundary to be hatched is not a closed boundary.

    (c) A mistake has been made in selecting the hatch pattern.

    (d) The wrong area to be hatched has been *picked*.

91. What action do you think desirable if the warning box appears?

92. If a **Preview** of a hatched area is not as wished, what steps can be taken to hatch as required?

    (a) The part of a drawing to be hatched must be redrawn.

    (b) A new hatch pattern must be selected.

    (c) The scale of the hatch pattern needs to be changed.

    (d) The angle of the hatch pattern must be changed.

93. What is the purpose of the **Advanced Options** when hatching?

94. Which hatch pattern is commonly used when hatching a section in an engineering drawing?

95. How are dimension styles set?

    (a) From the command line.

    (b) From the **Text Style** dialog.

    (c) From a **Dimension Style Manager** dialog.

    (d) By calling **ddim** and making settings in a dialog which appears.

96. Set a new text style in the **Text Style** dialog. Does text for the dimension style also change?

97. Which of these statements is correct?

    (a) Windows is an operating system for a computer.

    (b) Windows is the coprocessing system of a computer.

    (c) There is no need to have Windows loaded when working in AutoCAD.

    (d) AutoCAD 2004 can be run in Windows 95.

98. The original VGA system for monitor screens worked at:

    (a) 1024x768 pixels;

    (b) 800x600 pixels;

    (c) 1600x1200 pixels;

    (d) 3200x2400 pixels.

99. When constructing a drawing template **Limits** are defined by:

    (a) any sizes you wish to set;

    (b) the size in millimetres of the paper on which a drawing is to be printed;

    (c) with a lower limit of 0,0 and an upper limits of 1000,1000.

    (d) the number of pixels at which the monitor screen is working.

100. When setting limits the screen must be zoomed to ensure the limits are correct for the screen and the zoom prompt will be:

    (a) extents;

    (b) window;

    (c) dynamic;

    (d) all.

The Application of 2D CAD drawing

Dimensions

Simple linear dimensioning has already been dealt with in Chapter Three.

Notes

1. Remember that both the **A3_template.dwt** and the **A4_template.dwt** templates include a style of dimensioning already set up from the **Dimension Style** dialog.

2. There are two main methods by which dimensions can be included in a drawing:

   (a) By making use of appropriate dimension tools from the **Dimension** toolbar.

   (b) By using a command line method involving *entering* **dim**, *entering* appropriate abbreviations, followed by making suitable responses to the prompts which then appear.

The Dimension toolbar

Tools for dimensioning can be selected from the **Dimension** toolbar.

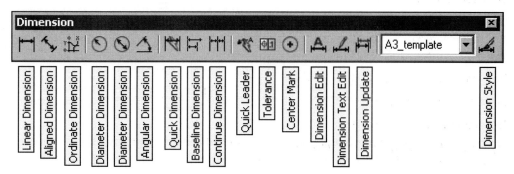

Example – dimlinear and dimradius

1. Open the **A3_template.dwt** template and construct the outline shown using the polyline tool.

2. *Left-click* the **Linear Dimension** tool icon.

Command:_dimlinear
Specify first extension line origin: *pick*
Specify second dimension line origin: *pick*
Specify dimension line location: *pick*
Dimension text = 120
Command:

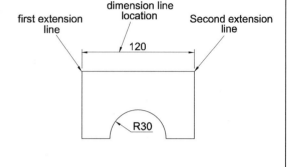

3. *Left-click* on the **Radius Dimension** tool.

Command:_dimradius
Select arc or circle: *pick* **the arc**
Dimension text = 30
Specify dimension line location: *pick* **a suitable point on the arc**
Command:

Other examples

Further examples of dimensioning using tools from the **Dimension** toolbar are shown below.

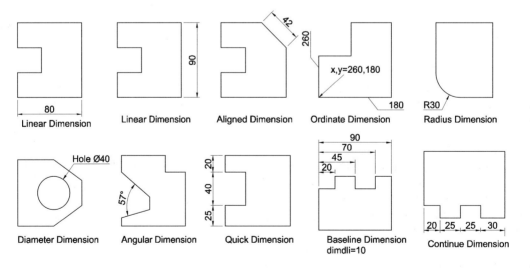

The examples above used the **A3_template** style of dimensioning. A variety of other dimension styles can be set in the **Dimension Style Manager**. Some examples of different styles are given below.

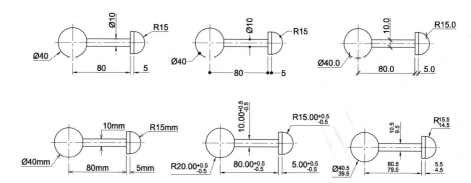

Dimensions from the Command line

Command: *enter* **dim** *right-click*
Dim: *enter* **hor (horizontal)** *right-click*
Specify first extension line origin: *pick*
Specify second dimension line origin: *pick*
Specify dimension line location: *pick*
Dimension text = 120
Command:
Dim:

First example – dimensions from the command line

1. **Open** the **A3_template.dwt** template. Construct the given drawing to the dimensions as shown.

2. At the command line:

Command: *enter* **dim** *right-click*
Dim: *enter* **hor** *right-click*
Specify first extension line origin: *pick*
Specify second dimension line origin: *pick*
Specify dimension line location: *pick*
Enter dimension text <50>: *right-click* **(accept 50)**
Dim: *right-click*
HORIZONTAL
Specify first extension line origin: *pick*
Specify second dimension line origin: *pick*
Specify dimension line location: *pick*
Enter dimension text <50>: *right-click*
Dim: *enter* **ve (vertical)** *right-click*
Specify first extension line origin: *pick*
Specify second dimension line origin: *pick*
Specify dimension line location: *pick*
Enter dimension text <30>: *right-click*
Dim:

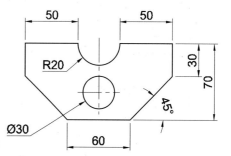

Continue in this manner until the drawing is completely dimensioned using abbreviations from the following list:

Other dimension abbreviations which can be used with Dim

l: leader

ra: radius

d: diameter

al: aligned

an: angular

cen: centre mark

Second example – drawing with tolerances

1. **Open** the **A3_template.dwt** template and construct the given drawing.

2. In the **Dimension Style Manger**, *left-click* on the **Modify** button and again on the **Tolerances** label.

3. Make *entries* in the **Tolerances** sub-dialog as shown.

4. Dimension the drawing.

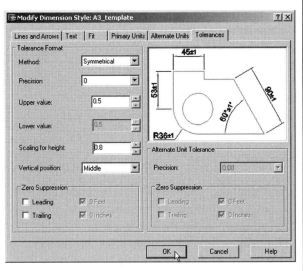

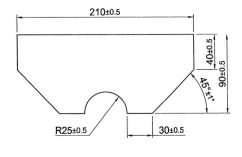

Layers

The use of layers is important when constructing technical drawings using any CAD software such as AutoCAD.

Layers can be thought of as similar to tracings in drawings constructed "by hand". Tracings lie one on top of each other when constructing drawings. They can be removed. Layers can be frozen or turned off. Tracings can be replaced in any order. Layers can be turned back on or thawed. When a tracing is on top it can be drawn on. Constructions can be added to the current layer in any CAD drawing.

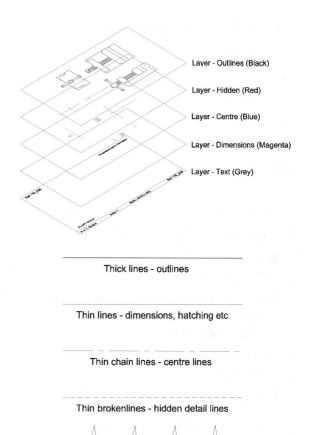

Layer - Outlines (Black)

Layer - Hidden (Red)

Layer - Centre (Blue)

Layer - Dimensions (Magenta)

Layer - Text (Grey)

Linetypes in technical drawings

Most technical drawings for mechanical engineering are made up from the linetypes as given. In other types of drawings, such as those for building and architecture, many other types of lines be used. In this chapter drawings constructed using the linetypes as shown are included.

Thick lines - outlines

Thin lines - dimensions, hatching etc

Thin chain lines - centre lines

Thin brokenlines - hidden detail lines

Thin chain lines - broken edges

A technical drawing

The drawing below was constructed on layers in the **A3_template.dwt** described in page 33. This is a three-view orthographic projection of a bench vice using the types of lines shown above.

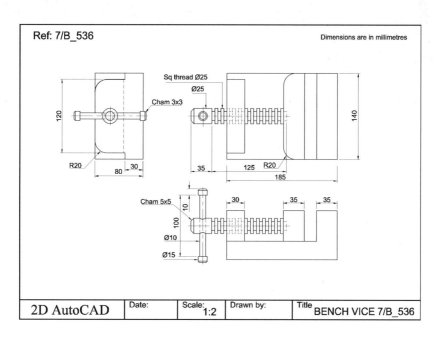

Ref: 7/B_536

Dimensions are in millimetres

Sq thread Ø25
Ø25
Cham 3x3
120
140
R20
80   30
35   125   R20
185

Cham 5x5
10
30   35   35
100
Ø10
Ø15

| 2D AutoCAD | Date: | Scale: 1:2 | Drawn by: | Title BENCH VICE 7/B_536 |

Layer Control popup list

Left-click on the arrow on the right of the **Layers** field in the **Object Properties** field and a popup list appears describing the layers in the **A3_template.dwt** template. To the left of each layer name are the layer control icons.

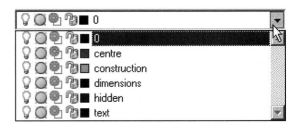

Layer Control icons

A *left-click* on the **Lock or Unlock a layer** icon changes its colour from yellow to grey and when grey that layer is off. A second *left-click* and the layer is turned on again. Similarly *left-clicks* on the other icons toggle the **Freeze or Thaw** and **Lock or Unlock** icon operations.

When a layer is locked, no object already drawn on the locked layer can be modified (e.g. erased), although objects can be added on a locked layer.

When a layer is turned off or frozen it cannot be brought on screen.

A *left-click* on a layer name makes that layer the current layer on which constructions can be made.

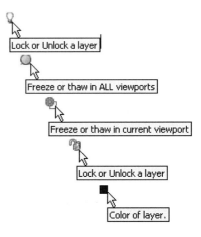

Construction lines

The **Construction Line** tool can be called either with a *left-click* on its icon in the **Draw** toolbar, by a *left click* on its name in the **Draw** drop down menu, or by *entering* **xl** or **xline** at the command line. Construction lines are of infinite length.

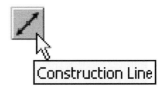

Command: *enter* **xl** *right-click*
XLINE Specify a point or [Hor/Ver/Ang/Bisect/Offset]:

First example – a drawing based on construction lines

1. **Open** the file **A3_template.dwt**.

2. *Left-click* to open the layer popup list

3. *Left-click* on **Construction** in the popup list to make the **Construction** layer current.

4. Call the **Construction Line** tool:

In the following sequences, *right-click* has not been included – only *enter* and the *x,y* coordinates.

Command: *enter* **xl** *right-click*
XLINE Specify a point or
[Hor/Ver/Ang/Bisect/Offset]: *enter* **v** *right-click*
Specify through point: **70,270** *right-click.*
Specify through point: **95,270** *right-click*
Specify through point: **135,270** *right-click*
Specify through point: **160,270** *right-click*
Specify through point: **250,270** *right-click*
Specify through point: **270,270** *right-click*
Specify through point: **290,270** *right-click*
Specify through point: *right-click*
Command: *right-click*
XLINE Specify a point or
[Hor/Ver/Ang/Bisect/Offset]: *enter* **h** *right-click*
Specify through point: **40,60** *right-click*
Specify through point: **40,120** *right-click*
Specify through point: **40,200** *right-click*
Specify through point: **70,160** *right-click*
Specify through point: *right-click*
Command:

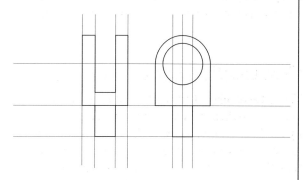

5. Makes layer **0** the current layer with a *left-click* on its name in layers the popup list. Basing the construction on the network of construction lines, construct the two views. Use **Polyline** set to **Width = 0.7**.

6. Turn the layer **Construction** off with a left-click on its **On/Off** icon in the layer popup list.

7. Make the layer **Centre** the current layer and add the centre lines, followed my making the layer **Hidden** current and adding hidden detail. Use **Polyline** set to **Width = 0.3**.

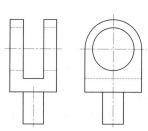

Second example – a simple orthographic projection

A pictorial view of a pivot arm from a machine is shown, together with a dimensioned two-view orthographic projection of the arm. This example describes the drawing of the two-view orthographic projection of the plate without the inclusion of the dimensions.

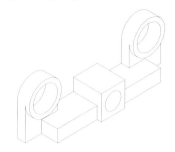

1. **Open** the **A3_template.dwt** template.

2. In the AutoCAD window layer **0** will automatically be the current layer.

3. On layer **0** and using the **Line**, **Arc** and **Circle**, **Polyline** and **Polyline Edit** tools, construct the two views as shown. Work to the given sizes, but do not attempt to include dimensions. When using the **Polyline** tool, draw the plines at a **Width** of **0.7**.

4. In the layers popup list, *left-click* on **Centre** to make the layer **Centre** current.

5. Add centre lines to the two views as required. Polylines of width 0.3.

6. In the layers popup list *left-click* on **Hidden** to make the layer **Hidden** current.

7. Add hidden detail lines to the two views as required. Polylines of width of 0.3.

8. In the layers popup list *left-click* on **Text** to make the layer **Text** current.

9. Using the **Polyline** tool construct a border and spaces for a title block.

10. Add text as shown.

11. In the layers popup list *left-click* on **Dimensions** to make layer **Dimensions** current.

12. Add the dimensions as shown.

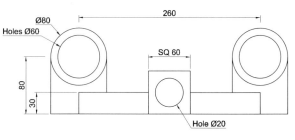

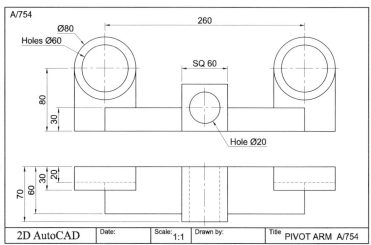

Types of drawings

Orthographic projection

Orthographic projection is one of the most common forms of technical drawing used to describe components and objects in the engineering and building industries. There are two methods of orthographic projection – first and third angle. In some countries third angle projection is most commonly used, but in many countries both angles of projection will be used. Some orthographic projections have already been shown in the earlier pages of this book.

Orthographic projections consist of views of the artefact being described in a technical drawing as seen from a variety of directions. Perspective is ignored in these views. In many cases three views are enough to fully describe the object, but many orthographic projections can be one, two, three or more views. The object of the projection is to describe the artefact as completely as possible. A projection of flat plate may only require one view, more complicated drawings may require many views. The views most frequently used are:

- **Front view** – view from the side most suitable as the front of the article.
- **Plan** – a view from above or from underneath.
- **End view** – a view from one side of the article.

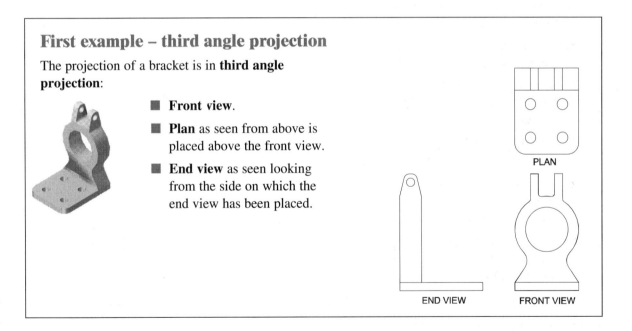

First example – third angle projection

The projection of a bracket is in **third angle projection**:

- **Front view**.
- **Plan** as seen from above is placed above the front view.
- **End view** as seen looking from the side on which the end view has been placed.

PLAN

END VIEW

FRONT VIEW

Notes

In working drawings the following are added:

■ **Centre lines** through all circles in all three directions.

■ **Hidden detail** lines.

■ **Dimensions**.

In addition a border is usually placed all around the drawing together with a title block containing details about the drawing. In the example below the drawing is within the borders of a template based on an A2 size sheet of drawing paper (840 mm × 594 mm) – **Limits** set to **840,594**.

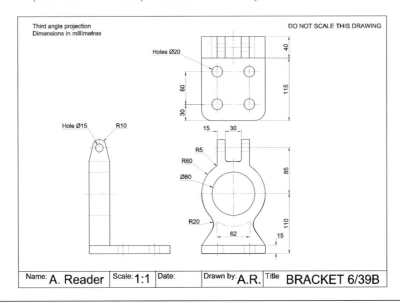

Second example – first angle projection

The projection of a spindle support is in **first angle projection**:

■ **Front view**.
■ **Plan** as seen from above is placed **below** the front view.
■ **End view** as seen looking from the side is placed on the other side from which the view is seen.

The drawing was constructed in a template based on an A2 sheet of drawing paper (594 mm × 420 mm). **Limits** set to **594,420**.

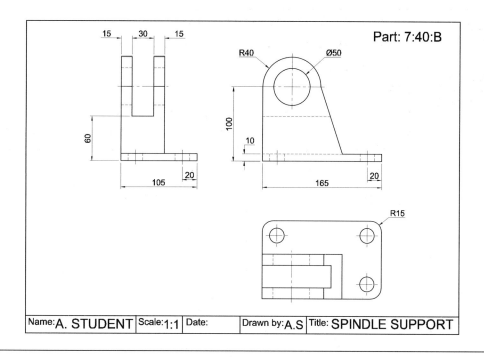

Isometric drawing

Isometric drawing is a 2D method of producing pictorial drawings, which resemble 3D views. Before commencing any isometric drawing the following preparations are necessary:

Set **Grid** to **10** and **Snap** to **5** in the **Snap** and **Grid** sub-dialog from the **Drafting Settings** dialog which is called with a *left-click* on **Drafting Settings …** in the **Tools** drop-down menu. To make these settings, first *left-click* in the **Isometric Snap** radio button to set it on (dot in button). Then *left-click* on the **OK** button of the dialog.

With the **A3_template.dwt** called to the screen, the AutoCAD window drawing area then appears with the grid dots arranged in an isometric fashion and with the cursor hair line arranged at isometric angles.

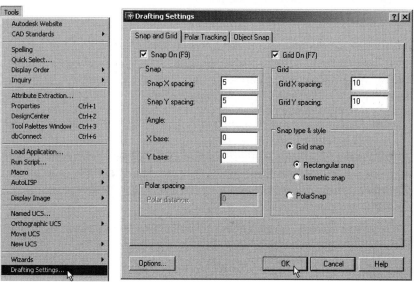

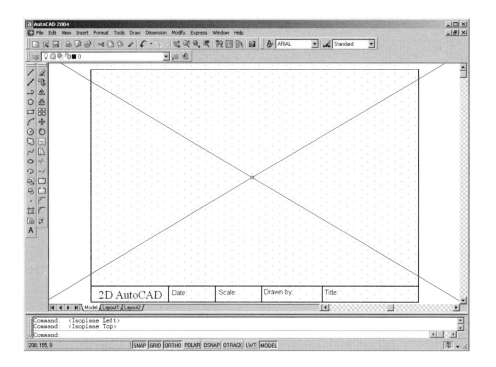

The Isoplanes

There are three **Isoplanes** – **Top**, **Left** and **Right**.
Isoplanes are toggled (changed from one to the other) either by pressing the key **F5** of the keyboard or pressing the **Ctrl** and **E** keys. As either of these actions is taken the cursor hair lines change between the three isoplane positions.

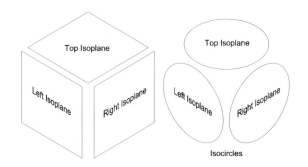

When an isometric circle is drawn in an isoplane, it will be an ellipse (an **Isocircle**). When the **Ellipse** tool is called with **Snap** set to the **Isometric** style (in the **Drafting Settings** dialog), the command line shows:

Command:_ellipse
Specify axis endpoint of ellipse or [Arc/Center/Isocircle]: *enter* **i (Isocircle)** *right-click*
Specify center of isocircle: *pick* **or** *enter* **coordinates**
Specify radius of isocircle or [Diameter]: *enter* **radius**
Command:

The isometric circle is formed in the Isoplane currently in operation.

First example

1. **Open** the **A4_template.dwt** template.

2. Set **Grid** (10) and **Snap** (5) in **Isometric** style.

3. Set Isoplane **Right**.

4. Using the **Polyline** tool set to **Width= 0.5** construct the given outline.

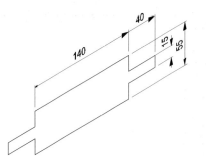

5. Set Isoplane **Left**.

6. Add plines as shown of length 70.

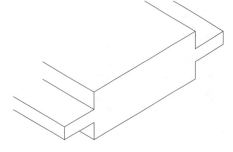

7. Set Isoplane **Top** and complete the isometric drawing as shown.

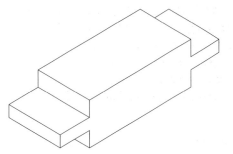

Second example

1. **Open** the **A4_template.dwt** template.

2. Set **Grid** and **Snap** in Isometric style.

3. Set Isoplane **Top**.

4. With **Polyline** set to **Width=0.5** construct the upper isometric rectangle as shown.

5. Set Isoplane as required to complete the drawing. All vertical dimensions are **10**.

6. To determine the centre point of the top of the isometric drawing, draw two lines from corner to corner.

7. Set Isoplane **Top**.

8. Call **Ellipse**:

   Command:_ellipse
   Specify axis endpoint of ellipse or [Center/Isocircle]: *enter* **i (Isocircle)** *right-click*
   Specify center of isocircle: *pick* **the intersection of the lines**
   Specify radius of isocircle or [Diameter]: *enter* **40** *right-click*
   Command:

9. Set Isoplane **Right**.

10. With **Copy,** copy the isocircle **10** vertically downwards.

11. Erase the two diagonal lines.

12. With the **Trim** tool trim the unwanted parts of the lower isocircle as shown.

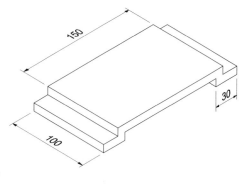

Third example

Open the **A4_template.dwt** template.

Stage 1: Construct an isometric "square" of 100 sides using the **Polyline** tool (**Width=1**).

Stage 2: With the **Chamfer** tool chamfer the corners 15x15. With **Copy**, copy the chamfered square back by **15**.

Stage 3: With **Trim**, trim unwanted parts of the isometric drawing.

Stage 4: Draw a pline from side to side 40 below the top edge of the front. Draw plines and isocircles as shown.

Stage 5: With **Copy,** copy the lines and isocircles vertically down by 15.

Stage 6: With **Trim,** trim away unwanted plines and parts of the isocircles.

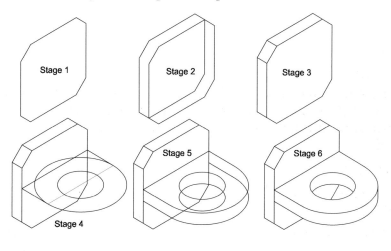

Assignments

1. Construct the given drawing using the **Polyline** tool. Then add dimensions showing a tolerance of **±0.05**.

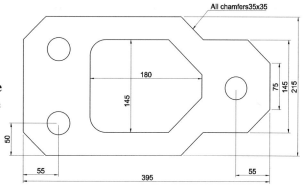

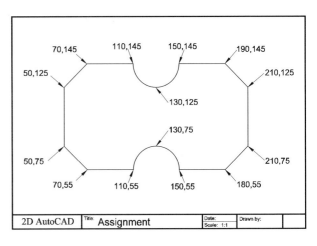

2. Open the **A3_template.dwt** template. Construct the given drawing to a scale of **1:2** and fully dimension the resulting drawing.

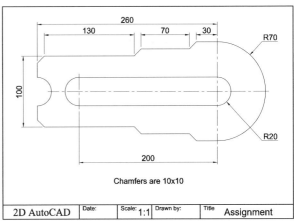

3. Open the **A4_template.dwt** template and construct the outline working to the given coordinates. Then fully dimension your resulting drawing.

4. A pictorial drawing of three components from a machine is shown. Several views of these three parts – **Block**, **Lever** and **Pin** are also given.

Construct a front view of the three parts in their working positions – with the lever held in its position within the block by the pin.

Use the tools **Polyline**, **Circle** and **Polyline Edit** to construct the required views.

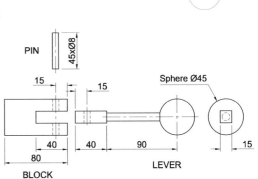

5. A pictorial drawing of a block is given and also a three-view orthographic projection of the block. Construct the given three views using the **Polyline** tool.

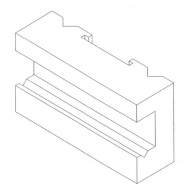

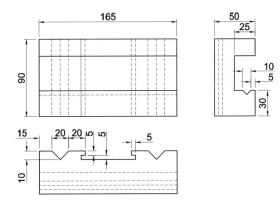

6. A pictorial drawing and a two-view drawing of a lever are given. Working with the tools **Polyline, Arc** and **Polyline Edit**, construct the two given views.

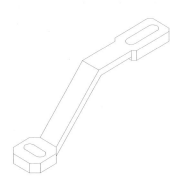

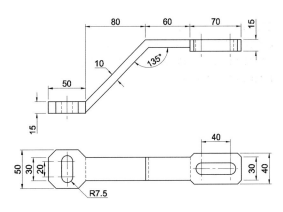

7. A pictorial drawing and a two-view drawing of a connecting part from a machine are given. Using the tools **Polyline**, **Arc**, **Circle** and **Polyline Edit** construct the two given views.

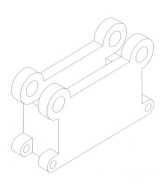

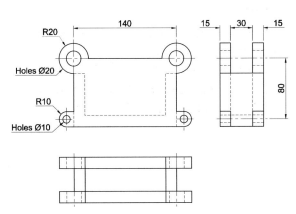

8. A pictorial drawing and a three-view drawing of a turning attachment are given. Construct the given three-view drawing using appropriate tools.

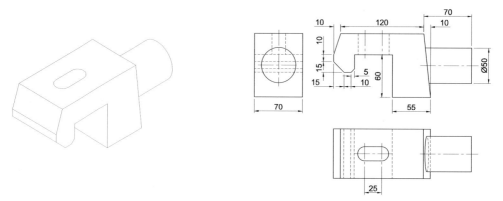

9. An isometric drawing and a three-view, first angle orthographic projection of a connecting device are given. From the given drawings construct a full scale isometric drawing as viewed from the left-hand end of the given front view. Add a three-view third angle orthographic projection of the device.

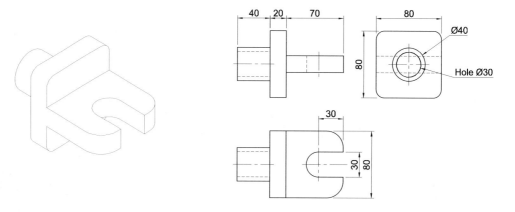

10. An isometric drawing and a two-view orthographic projection of a wheel from a vehicle are given. Construct the two given orthographic views as shown, but with the end view in section, the section plane being vertical and passing through the centre of the front view.

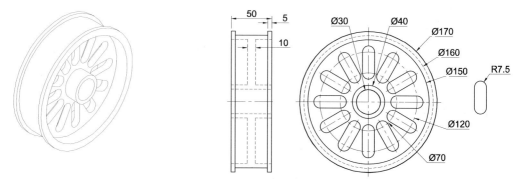

Assignments 10 to 12. An isometric drawing of an assembly consisting of four parts:

(a) A bracket.

(b) A rod which is of a size to fit into the holes of the bracket.

(c) A connector which can be pivoted with the bracket via the rod.

(d) A blade which is screwed into the screwed end of the connector.

Construct the following drawings:

10. Construct a three-view, first angle orthographic projection of the bracket from the details given in the first angle view shown.

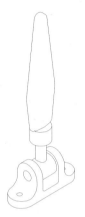

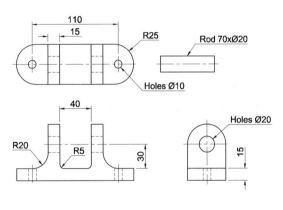

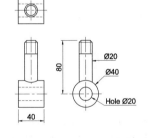

The drawing to the right shows a three-view orthographic projection of the connector holding the blade to the bracket

Notes

11. Construct a copy of the three-view orthographic projection of the given two views of the connector.

12. Construct a three-view first angle projection of the four parts of the assembly in their correct positions relative to each other.

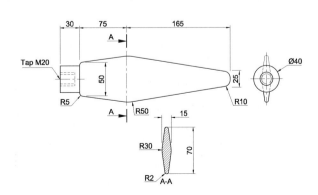

13. An isometric drawing and a three-view, first angle orthographic projection of a plastic lifting device are given. Construct a three-view, third angle projection of the device with the front viewing section.

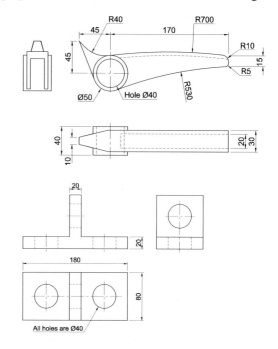

14. An orthographic projection of a simple bracket is shown. Construct a full size isometric drawing of the bracket.

All holes are Ø40

15. Working to the dimensions given with the drawing of a outdoors table, construct a full scale isometric drawing of the table.

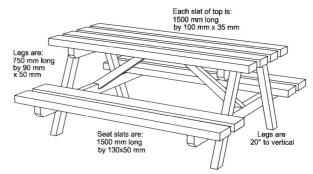

Each slat of top is:
1500 mm long
by 100 mm x 35 mm

Legs are:
750 mm long
by 90 mm
x 50 mm

Seat slats are:
1500 mm long
by 130x50 mm

Legs are
20° to vertical

Blocks and Inserts

Notes

1. Any previously saved AutoCAD drawing, or part of an AutoCAD drawing can be placed within another AutoCAD drawing by the use of the **Insert Block** tool.

2. Any AutoCAD drawing or part of an AutoCAD drawing can be saved as a separate drawing using the **Make Block** tool or the **Wblock** (write block) tool.

3. AutoCAD drawings can be inserted into other AutoCAD drawings from the **AutoCAD DesignCenter**.

4. AutoCAD drawings can be inserted into other AutoCAD drawings using the **External Reference** (**xref**) tool.

The Make Block tool

To call the **Make Block** tool, *left-click* on its tool icon in the **Draw** toolbar, or *left-click* on **Make...** in the **Block** sub-menu of the **Draw** drop-down menu, or *enter* **b** or **bmake** at the command line. When any of these alternatives are used, the **Block Definition** dialog appears.

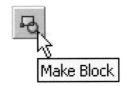
Make Block

Example – making blocks

1. **Open** the **A3_template.dwt** drawing template.

2. Construct the plan of a 2 m wide window.

Base point

3. Call **Make Block**. In the **Name:** field *enter* the name **window_2m**.

4. *Left-click* the **Pick Point** button. The dialog disappears.

5. *Left-click* at a selected point (the base point) of the window drawing. The **Block Definition** dialogue box reappears.

6. In the **Description** field *enter* a description of the block.

7. *Left-click* on the **Select objects** button:

   Command:_block

   Select objects: *window* the drawing **4 found**

   The dialog reappears. *Left-click* its **OK** button.

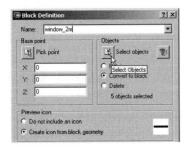

8. Repeat items **2** to **6** for the 4 other blocks as shown.

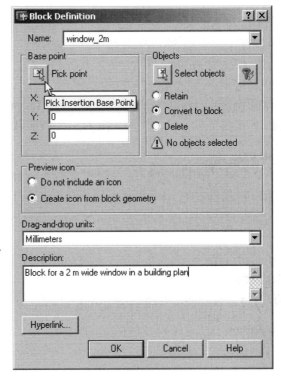

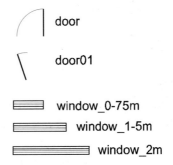
door

door01

window_0-75m

window_1-5m

window_2m

Notes

1. Many blocks can be drawn, saved and named in a drawing.

2. Blocks become part of the data in the drawing in which they were made.

3. Blocks created in this way can only be inserted in the drawing in which the blocks were made.

4. Each block is a single entity unless the **Explode** check box is on (tick in box) when the block is inserted by using the **Insert** tool (see page 109).

Written blocks (wblocks)

Any part of a drawing may be saved as a separate drawing by using the **wblock** command.

Command: *enter* **w** (wblock) *right-click*

The **Write Block** dialog appears. In the **File name and path** field *enter* **window_2m**. Then select an appropriate directory from a popup list appearing with a *left-click* on the button marked **....** *Left-click* on the **Pick Point** button.

WBLOCK Specify insertion base point: *pick*

The dialog reappears. *Left-click* the **Select Objects** button.

Select objects: *window* the drawing **4 found**

Select objects: *right-click*

The dialog reappears. *Left-click* its **OK** button.

Command:

A **WBLOCK Preview** window appears for a short time in the top-left-hand corner of the screen with a copy of the block.

The drawing is saved as a drawing in its own right. In this example its file name will be **C:\Build\window_2m.dwg**.

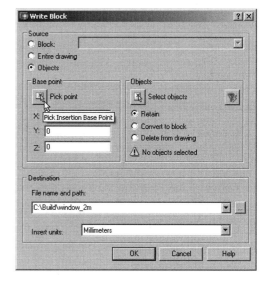

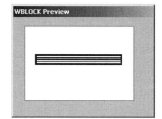

Notes

1. Do not confuse blocks with written blocks (wblocks). A block can only exist in the data of the drawing in which it was made. A written block is a new drawing in its own right and is not part of the data of another drawing.

2. Although the example above shows the saving of a building symbol (for a 2 m window plan), it must be understood that the size of a drawing saved as a block or as a wblock can be anything from a small part of a drawing to a drawing of any size.

The Insert tool

A block can be only be inserted into the drawing in which it was made by using the **Insert Block** tool. Any AutoCAD drawing (including those saved with the use of the **wblock** tool) can also be inserted into another drawing.

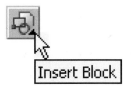

Insert Block

To call the **Insert Block** tool, *left-click* on its tool icon in the **Draw** toolbar, or *enter* **i** or **insert** at the command line. When either of these alternatives is made, the **Insert** dialog appears.

First example – inserting blocks into a drawing

1. **Open** the drawing in which the five blocks for the doors and windows have already been constructed.

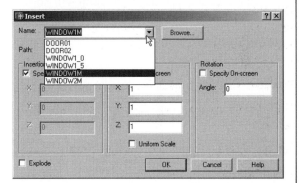

2. Use **Erase** to delete all the drawings of the blocks – but note the blocks will still be held in the data of the drawing file so can be called back to screen by using the **Insert Block** tool.

3. Construct the drawing below to the dimensions as shown, but do not include any of the dimensions.

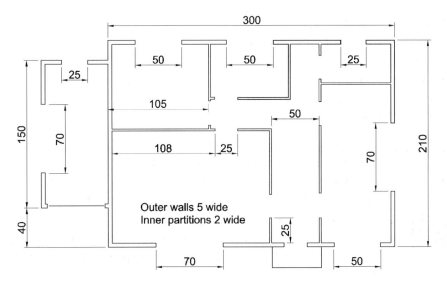

Outer walls 5 wide
Inner partitions 2 wide

4. Call the **Insert Block** tool. The **Insert** dialog appears. *Left-click* its **Browse...** button and from the **Select Drawing File** dialog which then appears select one of the five blocks for doors and windows. In the example below the **window_2m** block has been selected. *Left-click* the **OK** button of the dialog and the **window_2m** block appears on screen with its **Insertion base point** attached at the intersection of the cursor hairs, ready to be *dragged* to any position on screen under movement of the mouse. The command line shows:

Command:_insert
Specify insertion point or [Scale/X/Y/Z/Rotate/PX/PY/PZ/PRotate]: *pick* **point for the block**
Command:

and the **window_2m** block is placed in position.

5. Continue in this manner until all window and door spaces have had blocks inserted as shown in the drawing below. It will be necessary to rotate (using the **Rotate** option) some of the blocks to obtain suitable positions. Rotation will normally be through 90° or 270°.

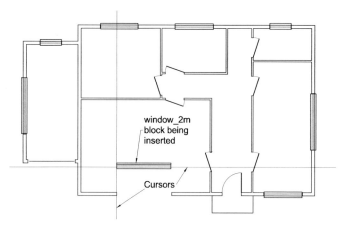

window_2m
block being
inserted

Cursors

Second example – inserting a wblock into a drawing

1. **Open** the **A3_template.dwt** template and construct the sectional drawing as shown.

2. **Save** the drawing to a suitable file name – for example **section.dwg**.

3. Construct the drawing of a rod and save as a **Wblock** to the name **rod.dwg**.

4. **Open** the drawing **section.dwg** and with the **Insert Block** tool, insert the rod into the section.

5. It will be necessary to use the **Trim** tool to trim the line crossing the rod at the base of the section.

6. The result is as shown.

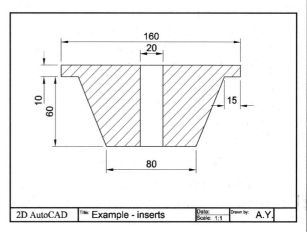

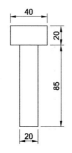

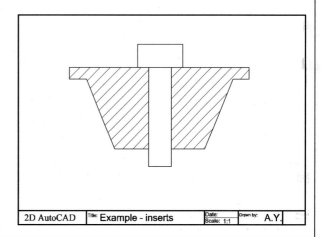

The External Reference tool

Example

Instead of saving the **rod.dwg** as a **Wblock**, save it as an **External Reference** or **xref** as follows:

1. **Open** the **section.dwg** drawing.

2. Call the **Xref** tool – either *left-click* on its icon in the flyout from the **Insert Block** tool icon in the **Draw** toolbar or *enter* **xref** or **xr** at the command line. The **Xref Manager** dialog appears.

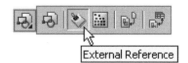

3. *Left-click* on the **Attach...** of the dialog, which causes the **Select Reference File** dialog to come on screen. From the dialog, select the file **rod.dwg**. *Left-click* on the dialog's **Open** button and another dialog (**External Reference**) appears showing the name **rod** in the **Name** field.

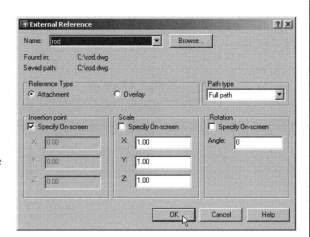

4. *Left-click* on the dialog's **OK** button and the rod appears on screen attached at the intersection of the cursor hairs of the AutoCAD screen. Place the rod in its place in the section and *right-click*.

5. So far the result appears to be the same as when the wblock **rod.dwg** was inserted.

6. Save the drawing with the xref to a new file name – e.g. **section02.dwg**.

7. **Open** the **rod.dwg** drawing and edit the drawing as shown. Save the revised drawing to a new name – e.g. **rod01.dwg**.

8. Now **Open** the **section02.dwg** and observe the changes in the xref **rod.dwg** when placed in the drawing as an **External Reference**.

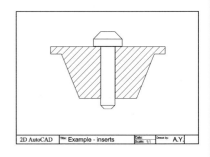

The AutoCAD DesignCenter

Many operators may prefer using the **AutoCAD DesignCenter** for the insertion of drawings or blocks. To call the **DesignCenter** *left-click* on its icon in the **Standard** toolbar, press the **Ctrl+2** keys of the keyboard, or *enter* **adcenter** at the command line.

DesignCenter (Ctrl+2)

Notes

In AutoCAD 2004 the **DesignCenter** is a palette. In previous AutoCAD 2000 and AutoCAD 2002 the **DesignCenter** is a window. Apart from this the method of using the **Design Center** is the same in all three releases of AutoCAD.

Drawings and/or blocks can be *dragged* from the **DesignCenter** lists into the AutoCAD drawing area. *Left-click* the **AutoCAD DesignCenter** tool icon. The **DesignCenter** appears. The **DesignCenter** consists of two parts, the left-hand side usually being a directories list, with the right-hand side showing the files in a selected directory. However the format of the **DesignCenter** can be changed. Try a *left-click* on the **Tree View Toggle** icon at the upper edge of the **DesignCenter** window and the window becomes a two parts become a single part. *Left-clicks* on other tool icons at the top of the **DesignCenter** window produce other formats of the window.

First example – dragging a drawing from the DesignCenter

1. Open the **DesignCenter** (*left-click* on its tool icon or press **Ctrl+2**) and the **DesignCenter** appears.

2. Hold the *pick* button of the mouse on a drawing file from the directory and files lists and *drag* into the AutoCAD drawing area. A small rectangular icon appears at the intersection of the cursor hairs. *Release* the *pick* button and the command line shows:

Command-INSERT Enter block name or [?]:
"C:\Concise Guide\Chap14\inserts\fig03.dwg"
Specify insertion point or [Scale/X/Y/Z/Rotate/PScale/PX/PY/PZ/PRotate]: *pick*
Enter X scale factor, specify opposite corner, or [Corner/XYZ] <1>: *right-click*
Enter Y scale factor <use X scale factor>: *right-click*
Specify angle: *right-click*
Command:

and the drawing appears in the AutoCAD drawing area.

Notes

Left-click on the **Preview** icon at the top of the **DesignCenter** and a small preview of the selected file appears at the bottom of the **DesignCenter**.

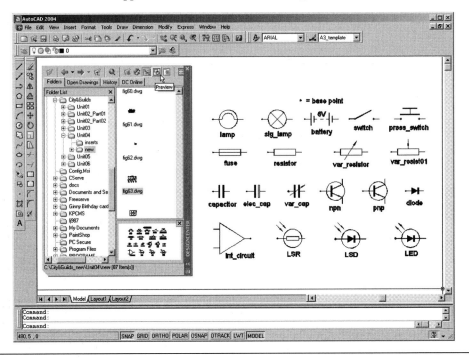

Second example – dragging a drawing from the DesignCenter

Instead of using the **Insert Block** tool to insert parts into a drawing as shown in the example on page 110, the **DesignCenter** can be used instead. By selecting the appropriate directory from the directories list in the **DesignCenter**, the symbol drawings for the parts of the building drawing can be *dragged* into their appropriate positions in a drawing in the AutoCAD window drawing area.

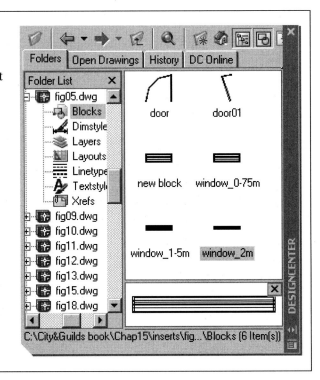

Printing and plotting

Introduction

The methods of printing/plotting a drawing described here are on the assumption that a computer is in use which has been set up to print or plot using default printers or plotters for that particular computer.

It does not matter whether the drawing is to be printed or plotted – the same tools and methods are used for either.

Prints or plots can be made from either the **Model Space** window (which has been used so far in this book) or from the **Paper Space** window. There is more about **Paper Space** on page 133. In the example given here the drawing is in **Model Space**.

To print or plot a drawing

To print a drawing on screen, settings will have to be made in the **Plot** dialog. There are two parts to this dialog – **Plot Device** and **Plot Settings**, which are brought on screen with *left-clicks* on the tabs at the top of the **Plot** dialog.

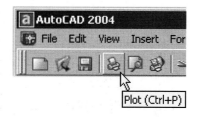

The Plot tool

The **Plot** dialog can be called with a *left-click* on **Plot** in the **File** drop-down menu, or with a *left-click* on the **Plot** icon in the **Standard** toolbar, or by pressing the **Ctrl+P** keys of the keyboard.

When the tool is called the **Plot** dialog appears on screen. The dialog is in two parts – **Plot Device** and **Plot Settings**.

Open the **Plot Device** dialog with a *left-click* on its tab and the **Plot Settings** with a *left-click* on its tab. In the example given the printer which has been selected is an **HP Laser Jet 1200**, brought into operation with a *left-click* on its name in the **Name** popup list. As this printer is an **A4** one, the settings in **Plot Settings** is for a **Paper Size** of **A4** sheet with a **Landscape** drawing orientation.

When the settings have been made in both dialogs, *left-click* on **Full Preview** button and a preview of the drawing within its A4 boundaries appears.

A *right-click* within the window brings up a right-click menu, from which choices may be made. A *left-click* on **Plot** in the menu and the drawing will be printed on the printer.

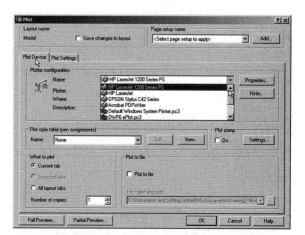

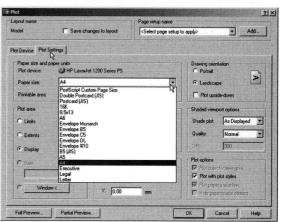

**Notes**

The drawing shown in the **Preview** window was constructed in an **A3_template.dwt** screen and can thus can only be printed/plotted full size on an **A3** sheet. In the example of printing shown here, the print was on an **A4** sheet (the **HP Laser Jet 1200** printer is an A4 printer), thus the drawing does not print full size (Scale 1:1). When using the template **A4_template.dwt** for constructing drawings, prints will be full size when printed to a printer such as a **HP Laser Jet 1200**.

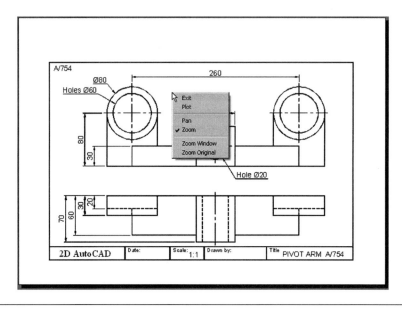

Using the Window> button

1. *Left-click* in the **Window** button in the **Plot dialog**.

2. The **Plot** dialog disappears and the command line requests windowing of the drawing in the AutoCAD window. Window the drawing.

3. *Left-click* on the **Full Preview** button. The preview window appears showing the position of the drawing as it will be plotted on the drawing sheet.

4. If satisfied, *right-click* and from the menu *left-click* on **Plot**. The drawing prints.

5. If not satisfied with the appearance of the preview *right-click* and *pick* **Exit** from the menu. Then reset any of the parameters from the dialog which might improve the position and size of the plot.

It is advisable to experiment with different settings available in the **Plot** dialogs.

Different printers or plotters

Different printers or plotters may be attached to the computer in use. It does not matter which type is used, the methods of printing or plotting a drawing will be the same as described above.

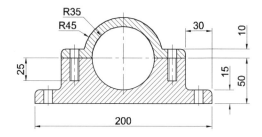

Assignments

1. Construct this front sectional view of a spindle bearing to the given dimensions. Save the drawing to a suitable file name

   Then construct the front view of the bolt and save it as a wblock.

   Reopen the front sectional view of the bearing and insert the blocks in appropriate positions in the sectional views.

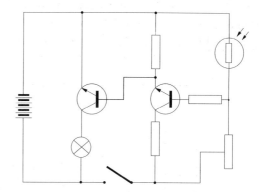

2. In an **A3_template.dwt** template construct the electronics symbols as shown, saving each as a wblock in a directory named **electronics** using the file names underneath each symbol.

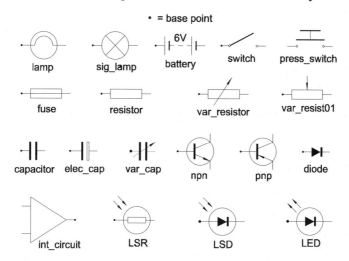

3. **Open** the A3_template.dwt template. Then, using the **Insert Block** tool, construct this electronics circuit from your directory **electronics** using polylines to connect the symbols to form a complete circuit drawing.

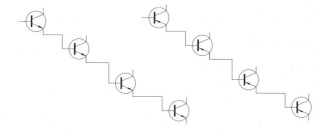

4. Part of an electronics circuit includes a chain of **npn** transistors arranged as shown in the drawing in exercise 3. The symbols had been inserted as **xrefs**. Construct the left-hand drawing as shown. Use the wblock drawing of an **npn** transistor symbol saved for exercise **2**.

Then recall the **npn** symbol and change it to a **pnp** transistor symbol. Save this new drawing and reopen the original circuit drawing which included the **npn** transistor symbols. The result should be as in the right-hand drawing below.

5. Open any of the drawings saved from working examples and assignments and print or plot them.

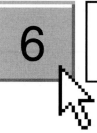

6 | Chapter Six

Drawing modification

Mirror tool

When AutoCAD is loaded, the **Modify** toolbar is usually *docked* against the **Draw** toolbar on the left-hand edge of the AutoCAD window. One of the tools from the **Modify** toolbar is **Mirror**.

To call the **Mirror** tool *left-click* on its icon in the **Modify** toolbar, or on its name in the **Modify** drop-down menu, or *enter* **mi** or **mirror** at the command line.

First example – The Mirror tool

1. Construct the left-hand drawing.

2. Call the **Mirror** tool:

Command:_mirror
Select objects: *pick*
Specify opposite corner: *pick*
Select objects: *right-click* **3 found**
Specify first point of mirror line: *pick*
Specify second point of mirror line: *pick*
Delete source objects [Yes/No] <N>: *right-click*
Command:

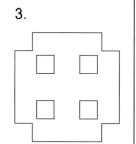

Second example – The Mirror tool

1. Construct drawing **1**.

2. Call the **Mirror** tool.

3. Mirror the drawing **1** horizontally – drawing **2**.

4. Then mirror drawing **2** vertically – drawing **3**.

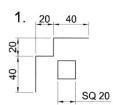

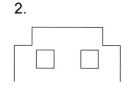

Notes

When using **Mirror** on drawings containing text, the variable **MIRRTEXT** must be set:

Command: *enter* **mirrtext** *right-click*
Enter new value for MIRRTEXT <1>: *enter* **0** *right-click*
Command:

This is text with MIRRTEXT = 1   ↑ = TXƎTЯЯIM ʜɟiw ɟxǝɟ ƨi ƨiʜT
TʜiƨꙆ ƨi ɟǝxɟ ʍiʜɟ ΜIЯЯꞀƎXꞀ = ↓

This is text with MIRRTEXT = 0 This is text with MIRRTEXT = 0
This is text with MIRRTEXT = 0

The Copy Object tool

To call the **Copy Object** tool, *left-click* on its icon in the **Modify** toolbar, or its name in the **Modify** drop-down menu, or *enter* **cp** or **copy** at the command line:

Copy Object

Command_copy
Select objects: *pick* **object(s)** *right-click*
Specify base point or displacement or
[Multiple]:

First example – single copy

1. **Open** template **A4_template.dwt** and construct the left-hand drawing.

2. Call the **Copy Object tool:**

Command_copy
Select objects: *pick* **object 1 found**
Select objects: *right-click*
Specify base point or displacement or [Multiple]: *pick*
Specify second point of displacement or <use first point as displacement>: *pick*
Command:

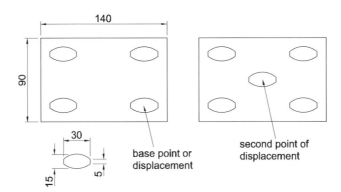

Second example – multiple copies

1. **Open** the **A4_template.dwt** and construct the left-hand drawing.

2. Call the **Copy Object** tool:

Command_copy
Select objects: window the objects 2 found
Select objects: *right-click*
Specify base point or displacement or [Multiple]: *enter* **m** *right-click*
Specify base point: *pick*
Specify second point of displacement or <use first point as displacement>: *pick*
Specify second point of displacement or <use first point as displacement>: *pick*
Specify second point of displacement or <use first point as displacement>: *pick*
Specify second point of displacement or <use first point as displacement>: *pick*
Specify second point of displacement or <use first point as displacement>: *right-click*
Command:

3. The right-hand drawing shows the result.

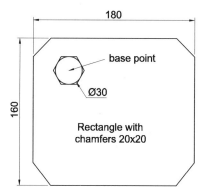
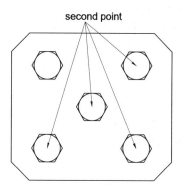

The Move tool

To call the **Move** tool, *left-click* on its icon in the **Modify** toolbar, or on its name in the **Modify** drop-down menu, or *enter* **m** or **move** at the command line.

Command:_move
Select objects: *pick*
Select objects: *right-click*
Specify base point or displacement: *pick*
Specify second point of displacement or <use first point as displacement>: *pick*
Command:

Example – Move

1. **Open** the **A4_template.dwt** template. Draw the left-hand drawing.

2. Call Move:

Command:_move
Select objects: *pick* **the pline**
Select objects: *right-click*
Specify base point or displacement:
pick
Specify second point of displacement or
<use first point as displacement>: *pick*
Command:

3. The result is given in the right-hand drawing.

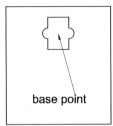

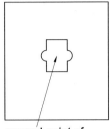

base point

second point of
displacement

The Stretch tool

To call the **Stretch** tool *left-click* on its icon in the
Modify toolbar, or on its name in the **Modify**
drop-down menu, or *enter* **s** or **stretch** at the
command line.

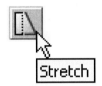

Stretch

Stretch – two examples

1. **Open** the **A3_template.dwt** template.

2. Construct the top left-hand drawing.

3. **Multiple Copy** the drawing two times.

4. Call the **Stretch** tool:

Command:_stretch
Select objects to stretch by crossing
window or crossing polygon ...
Select objects: *enter* **c** *right-click*
Specify first corner: *pick* **Specify**
opposite corner: *pick* **2 found**
Specify first point or displacement: *pick*
Specify second point of displacement or
<use first point as displacement>: *pick*
Command:

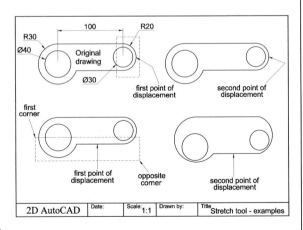

As can be seen from these two examples, if an attempt is made to **Stretch** a circle, the attempt will fail, but arcs can be acted upon by the tool

Notes

The Rotate tool

To call the **Rotate** tool, *left-click* on its icon in the **Modify** toolbar, or on its name in the **Modify** drop-down menu, or *enter* **ro** or **rotate** at the command line.

Rotate – five examples

1. **Open** the **A3_template.dwt** template.

2. Construct the top-left-hand drawing.

3. Using the **Rotate** tool, follow the directions in the drawing – i.e. with **Copy** copy the top left-hand drawing, then use **Rotate** at the angle shown.

4. Call the **Rotate** tool:

Command_rotate
Current positive angle in UCS: ANGDIR=counterclockwise ANGBASE=0
Select objects: *pick* top left of drawing Specify opposite corner: *pick*
Select objects: *right-click*
Specify base point: *pick*
Specify rotation angle or [Reference]: *enter* **30** *right-click*
Command:

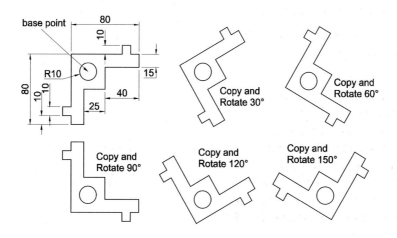

The Inquiry toolbar

Right-click in any toolbar on screen and from the toolbar menu which appears *pick* **Inquiry**. The toolbar comes on to the screen.

First example – the Distance tool

To call the **Distance** tool, either *left-click* on its tool icon in the **Inquiry** toolbar or enter **di** or **dist** at the command line. When called the distance between two points must be *picked* – an example is shown.

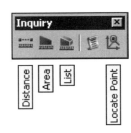

Notes

1. In this example the command window has been *dragged* from its usual place at the bottom of the AutoCAD window into the drawing area. In AutoCAD 2004 the command "window" is a palette when it is away from its default position. In earlier releases of AutoCAD, such as AutoCAD 2000 and AutoCAD 2002, the command window was a true Windows' window.

2. If the two points *picked* in response to the **Distance** prompts are at an angle, the size of the angle is given in the response.

```
Command: '_dist Specify first point:  Specify second point:
Distance = 205,  Angle in XY Plane = 0,  Angle from XY Plane = 0
Delta X = 205,  Delta Y = 0,  Delta Z = 0
Command:
```

Second example – the Area tool

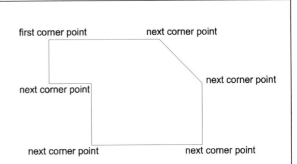

1. Construct any outline such as that shown.

2. Call the **Area** tool either with a *left-click* on its tool icon in the **Inquiry** toolbar or by *entering* **area** at the command line.

Command:_area
Specify first corner point or
[Object/Add/Subtract]: *pick* **first point**
Specify next corner point or press ENTER for total: *pick* **next point**

and so on until the final point is *picked:*

Specify next corner point or press ENTER for total: *right-click*
Area = 16850. Perimeter = 571.
Command:

Notes

1. If **o** for **Object** had been *entered* as a response to the first line at the command line and the outline was a polyline, by *picking* anywhere on the pline, the total area would have been given immediately.

2. The area figure is in square units, the unit being a coordinate unit. To translate the area figure into other units, the scale of the drawing must be known. As this example was constructed in an **A3_template.dwt** screen, the given area figure is in square millimetres.

Third example – the List tool

1. Taking the outline given in the **Area** example.

2. Call the **List** tool, either with a *left-click* on its tool icon in the **Inquiry** toolbar or by *entering* **li** or **list** at the command line.

Command:_list
Select objects: *pick* **the outline 1 found**
Select objects: *right-click*

```
AutoCAD Text Window                              _|□|×
Edit
Command:
LIST
Select objects: 1 found
Select objects:                          Recent Commands  ▶
                                         Copy
            LWPOLYLINE  Layer: "0"       Copy History
                   Space: Model space    Paste
            Handle = 106                 Paste To Cmdline
       Closed
Constant width        0                  Options...
         area    16850
    perimeter     571
      at point  X=      85   Y=    205   Z=         0
      at point  X=     215   Y=    205   Z=         0
      at point  X=     265   Y=    155   Z=         0
      at point  X=     265   Y=     85   Z=         0
      at point  X=     135   Y=     85   Z=         0
      at point  X=     135   Y=    155   Z=         0
      at point  X=      85   Y=    155   Z=         0
Command:
```

and an **AutoCAD Text Window** appears with the list for the *picked* object.

Notes

1. A right-click menu automatically appears with the window. It is worth experimenting with *picking* each of the items in this menu to show how much information can be gained about a drawing from calling the **List** tool.

2. Any of the objects in a drawing can be *picked*, or all by windowing a whole drawing. The details given in the text window can then be extensive.

Fourth example – the Locate Point tool

To call the **Locate Point** tool, either *left-click* its tool icon in the **Inquiry** toolbar or *enter* **id** at the command line.

Command:_id Specify point *pick* **a point in the AutoCAD window X = 190 Y = 60 Z = 0**
Command:

The coordinates of any point in the AutoCAD window can be shown using the tool.

Fifth example – The Divide tool and Points

1. In the **Format** drop-down menu *left-click* **Point Style**. The **Point Style** dialog appears. *Pick* one of the point styles, followed by *clicking* the **OK** button of the dialog.

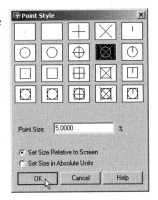

2. Draw a pline of any length.

3. Call the **Divide** tool, *enter* **div** or **divide** at the command line.

Command:_divide
Select objects to divide: *pick* **the pline**
Enter number of segments or [Block]:
enter **15** *right-click*
Command:

and the chosen point style appears at 15 points along the pline.

4. By saving a drawing as a block some interesting divisions can be constructed using the **Block** option of the **Divide tool**. The example given below shows a small heart-shaped block dividing a circle at 20 points.

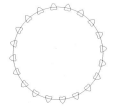

Grips

Grips are small *pick* boxes that appear at points on any object which has been *picked* when no tool is in operation. **Grips** will not operate unless the set variable **Grips** is set on (to **1**).

To set variable GRIPS:

Command: *enter* **grips** *right-click*
Enter new value for GRIPS <0>: *enter* **1** *right-click*
Command:

Example

1. Open the **A3_template.dwt** template.

2. Construct the outline as given to any suitable size using the **Polyline** tool. *Pick* the outline. **Grips** *pick* boxes appear around the *picked* object as shown.

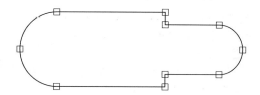

3. *Pick* one of the grips. It changes colour and the command line shows:

Command:
** STRETCH **
Specify stretch point or [Base point/Copy/Undo/eXit]: press the Return key
** MOVE **
Specify move point or [Base point/Copy/ Undo/eXit]: press the Return key
** ROTATE **
Specify rotation angle or [Base point/Copy/Undo/Reference/eXit]: press the Return key
** SCALE **
Specify scale factor or [Base/ point/Copy/ Undo/Reference/eXit}: press the Return key
** MIRROR **
Specify second point or [Base point/Copy/Undo/eXit}:

This means that when grips are showing on a selected object five of the **Modify** tools can be called by continuously pressing the **Return** key.

The result of accepting any one of the five tools after *picking* one of the **Grips** is shown in the following drawing.

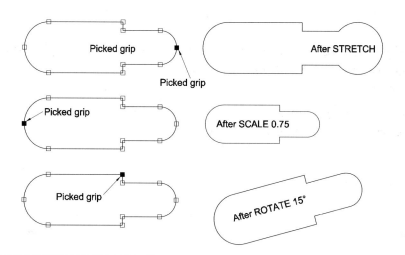

DXF and Raster files

DXF files

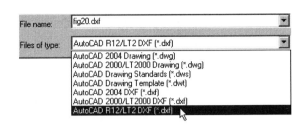

Files with the extension ***.dxf** are of Autodesk (the publishers of AutoCAD) design. However ***.dxf** files can be used by the majority of CAD software applications. A drawing constructed in most CAD software can be saved as a DXF file. Such DXF files can then be opened in other CAD software.

To save a file to this format, from the **File** drop-down menu select **Save As...** and in the **Save Drawing As** dialog, *left-click* on the arrow to the right of the **Files of type** field and in the popup list which then appears, *pick* **AutoCAD 2000 DXF (*.dxf)** and after *entering a* suitable file name in the **File name** field, l*eft-click* on the **Save** button.

The saved file can now be opened in most other CAD software applications including AutoCAD.

Raster files

Bitmaps of the file types such as ***.bmp**; **pcx**; **jpg**; **tga** and many other image files can be inserted into AutoCAD drawings as in the example which follows:

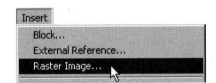

1. *Left-click* on **Raster Image...** in the **Insert** drop down menu.

2. The **Select Image File** dialog appears. *Left-click* on the arrow to the right of the **Files of type** field and from the popup list select **BMP, (*.bmp, *.rle, *.dib)**.

3. Select the file name to be inserted into the drawing – in this case the bitmap image shown on page 96 and *left-click* the **Open** button. The **Image** dialog opens showing the selected file in its **Name** field.

4. *Left-click* the dialog's **OK** button the command line shows:

Command:_imageattach
Specify insertion point (0,0): *pick* **a point on screen**
Specify scale factor <1:1>: *enter* **a suitable scale factor**
Command:

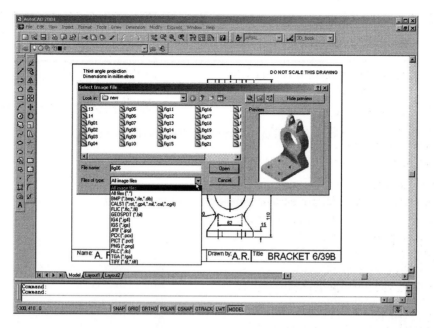

5. The image can now be placed in any suitable position as required within a drawing on screen. The drawing with its raster image can now be printed or plotted and/or saved to a file name as a ***.dwg** file.

The Properties palette

In AutoCAD 2004, the **Properties** dialog is in palette form. In earlier releases of AutoCAD it was in a windows form. To open the **Properties** palette, with a drawing on screen, *left-click* on the **Properties** tool icon in the **Standard** toolbar, or *enter* **properties** at the command line or *double-click* on any object in a drawing on screen, No matter which method is adopted, the **Properties** window appears *docked* against the left-hand side of the AutoCAD window.

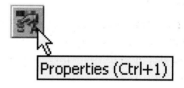

Objects in an AutoCAD drawing are affected by the following eight properties:

1. The **Make Object's Layer Current** tool (**Standard** toolbar), use of which will change the layer on which an object was constructed.

2. The current layer of the object.

3. Any previous layer on which the object was constructed.

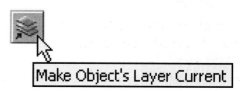

4. The object's default layer.

5. The colour of the object.

6. The linetype of the object.

7. The lineweight of the object.

8. The Plot style of the object.

These properties can be checked and/or changed from the **Properties** window.

First example – checking properties of a dimension

1. With a drawing in the AutoCAD window *double-click* on a dimension and the **Properties** palette appears.

2. The name of the type of object selected appears in a field at the top of the **Properties** palette.

3. *Left-click* on the **Select Objects** button at the top of the **Properties** palette, then on the tab marked **Text**.

4. In the list which appears, select **Style**.

5. An arrow appears in the **Style** field. *Left-click* on the arrow and in the popup list *Left-click* on **Standard**. The text in the 110 dimension in the drawing changes from **ARIAL** to **Standard** text style.

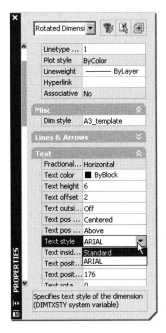

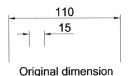

Original dimension

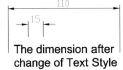

The dimension after change of Text Style

Notes

The properties of any object in a drawing on screen can be described and/or changed in the **Properties** window.

Attributes

Attributes can be included with drawings, which can then be saved and inserted into other drawings as blocks together with the attributes. Once inserted into another drawing the attributes can be edited. An example follows.

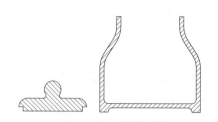

Example – an attribute

1. Construct the drawing of a sectional view through a container to any dimensions and save to a suitable file name.

2. Construct the second drawing of a sectional drawing through a lid for the container.

3. At the command line:

Command: _enter_ ddattdef

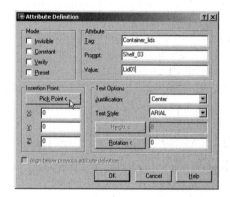

the **Attribute Definition** dialog appears. Make entries in the **Tag**, **Prompt** and **Value** fields as shown. Set the **Justification** field in the **Text Options** area of the dialog to **Center**.

4. _Left-click_ on the **Pick Point** button. The dialog disappears.

5. _Pick_ a point for the attribute tag on the drawing. The dialog reappears. _Left-click_ its **OK** button. The tag appears at the point picked on the drawing.

6. Save the drawing with its attribute to a suitable file name.

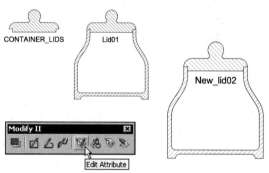

7. Open the sectional drawing of the container and insert the lid drawing which appears in its position showing the attribute value.

8. Bring the **Modify II** toolbar on screen and _left-click_ on the **Edit Attribute** tool icon. The command line shows:

Command:_eattedit
Select a block: _pick_ the block

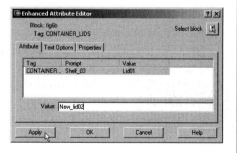

The **Enhanced Attribute Manager** dialog appears.

9. In the dialog _enter_ **New_lid02** in the **Value** field, followed by a _left-click_ on the **Apply** button, followed by another _left-click_ on the dialog's **OK** button.

10. The attribute value changes in the drawing.

Assignments

1. Using the **Mirror** tool construct the two main drawings working to the given dimensions.

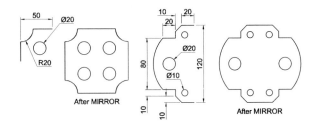

2. Construct drawing **1** as shown. From that drawing complete the exercise as given in drawing **2**. Use Circle, Polyline, Array, Trim and Pedit.

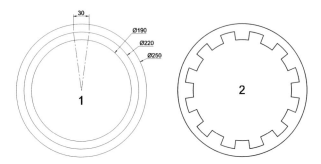

3. Construct drawing **1** as given. Using drawing **1** as a basis, complete the exercise as shown in drawing **2**. Use **Circle**, **Line**, **Array**, **Trim** and **Edit Polyline**.

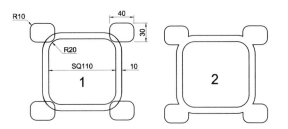

4. Construct drawing **2** to the dimensions given in drawing **1** using **Rectangle** (with **Fillet** set as shown and **Width = 1**).

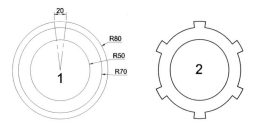

5. Construct the main drawing as given. Using **Grips** first stretch the central object by **20** units, followed by calling **Undo**. Then again using **Grips** rotate the central object by **15°**, followed by **Undo**. Then using **Grips** scale the central object to **0.5**.

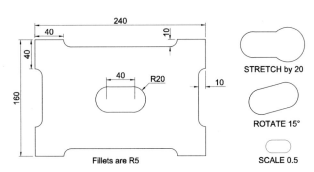

6. **Open** any previously saved drawing. Save the drawing as a DXF file. Close the drawing and **Open** the DXF file previously saved. Are there any differences?

7. **Open** the isometric drawing made for the second example (page 100). This drawing was constructed using a polyline of **0.5** width. Open the **Properties** window and edit the main outline of the drawing to a polyline of a width of **2**.

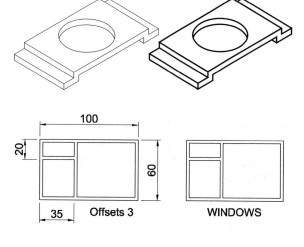

8. Construct the left-hand drawing of a window to the dimensions as shown. Add an attribute:

Tag: **Windows**;
Prompt: **Centre**;
Value: **Window_1m_opening**.
Save the drawing with its attribute to a suitable file name.

Then:

(a) In a new template construct the outline of a wall of a house to any suitable size.

(b) Insert the window drawing with its attribute.

(c) Using **Edit Attribute** tool change the attribute value to **Window_1.5m_closed**.

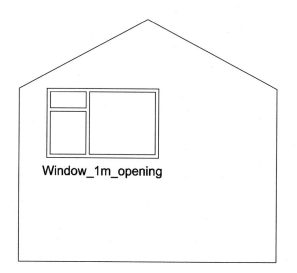

Window_1m_opening

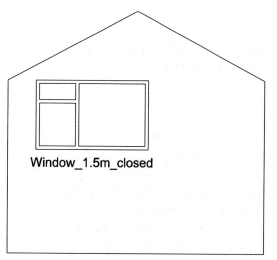

Window_1.5m_closed

9. Construct drawing **1** as shown. From that drawing complete the exercise as given in drawing **2**.

Use **Circle**, **Polyline**, **Array**, **Trim** and **Pedit**.

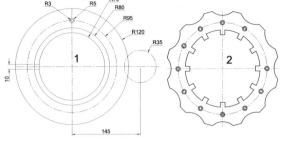

10. Construct the left-hand drawing to the dimensions as given using **Polyline**, **Circle**, **Trim** and **Pedit** tools. **Multiple Copy** the drawing three times.

Using the **Rotate** tool rotate the three copies to the angles as given with the drawing.

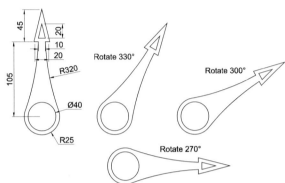

Mspace and Pspace

All the drawings in this book have so far been constructed in Model Space (Mspace). Drawings can either be created within a drawing template, which includes borders and a title block such as those described in pages 36 to 37, or in templates without such borders and title block. Templates can be constructed and saved in either Mspace or in Pspace (Paper Space). Drawings constructed in Model Space can then be printed or plotted from either Mspace or from Pspace.

Example

The given drawing shows the answers to assignments 2 and 3 from page 62. This drawing was described as being constructed in Model Space in the template A4_template.dwt. To print the drawing from Pspace: *Left-click* on the tab labelled **Layout1** in the bottom left-hand corner of the AutoCAD window. The drawing appears in PSpace.

The drawing can be printed or plotted from Pspace (see pages 115 to 116).

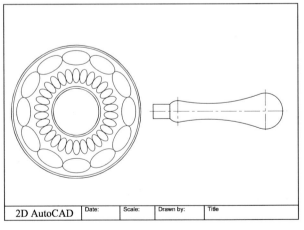

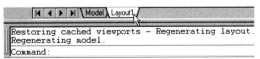

The layer Psvports

The layers of the template **A4_template.dwt** include the layer Psvports of a colour cyan. If the drawing shown above had been constructed in this template and before the **Layout1** tab was *clicked*, or the layer **Psvports** made the current layer, the drawing would appear in Pspace with a layer border coloured cyan outside the actual drawing border. This is shown in the illustration on the right.

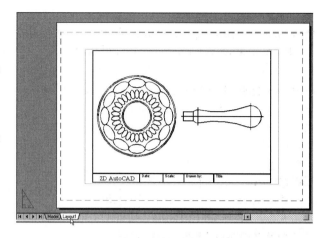

If required this cyan coloured border can be turned off with a *left-click* on the on/off icon in the layer popup list. With the layer turned off, the cyan border no longer shows.

Modifications and entries in the title block can only now be added to the drawing while in Pspace if the **PAPER** tab in the status bar at the bottom of the AutoCAD window is *clicked*. With a *click* on this tab, its title changes to **MODEL**. Additions and changes can then be made to the drawing and text can be added to the title block.

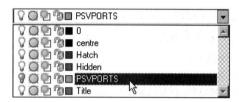

Modifications to the drawing cannot take place while the tab is at **PAPER**.

Make any changes to the drawing which may be necessary and complete the title block.

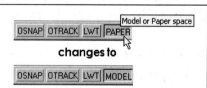

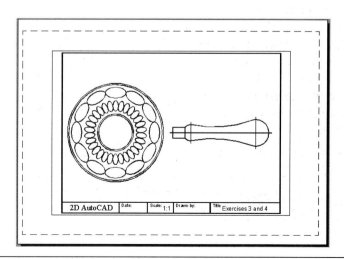

Linetype scale

When the A3_template.dwt was set up, the linetype scale (**ltscale**) was set to 30. This setting affects linetypes such as hidden lines and centre lines. To change the linetype scale, at the command line:

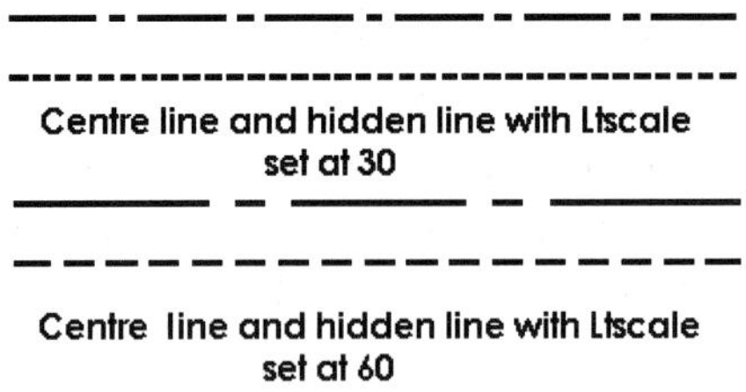

Centre line and hidden line with Ltscale set at 30

Centre line and hidden line with Ltscale set at 60

Command: *enter* **ltscale** *right-click*
Enter new linetype scale factor <30>:
enter **60** *right-click*
Regenerating model.
Command

The Change command

Another method of changing features in a drawing is to use the command **change** as follows:

Command: *enter* **change** *right-click*
Select objects: *pick* **the object requiring changing**
Select objects: *right-click*
Specify change point or [Properties]: *enter* **p (Properties)** *right-click*
Enter property to change [Color/Elev/LAyer/LType/Ltscale/LWeight//Thickness]: *enter* **c (Color)** *right-click*
New color [Truecolor/COlbook] <BYLayer>: *enter* **red** *right-click*
Enter property to change [Color/Elev/LAyer/LType/Ltscale/LWeight//Thickness]: *right-click*
Command:

and the selected object changes colour to red.

In a similar manner the properties of objects can be changed with regard to the layer on which they have been constructed; the linetype of lines; the linetype scale.

To change text

1. In an A3_template.dwt *enter* some text – in the example this is **Bolt M10x1.5**.

2. At the command line:

Command: *enter* **change** *right-click*
Select objects: *pick* **the object requiring changing**
Select objects: *right-click*
Specify change point or [Properties]: *left-click* **the text**
Enter new text style <ARIAL>: *enter* **times** *right-click*
Specify new rotation angle <0>: *right-click*
Enter new text <Bolt M10x1.5>: *enter* **Bolt 12x1** *right-click*
Command:

Bolt M10x1.5

Bolt 12x1

and the text changes to the new text style and new text.

The Properties toolbar

Colour, linetype and line width of objects in a drawing can be changed with the aid of the **Properties** palette (window in previous AutoCADs). Or they can be changed from the **Properties** toolbar. Some operators prefer to have the **Properties** toolbar *docked* just below the **Standard** toolbar at the top of the AutoCAD window in order to be able to change some objects properties from the toolbar.

To change colour, linetype or line width, *left-click* on the object to be changed. Grips appear on the objects (see page 126). Then select the required new property for the object from the relevant popup list in the **Properties** toolbar.

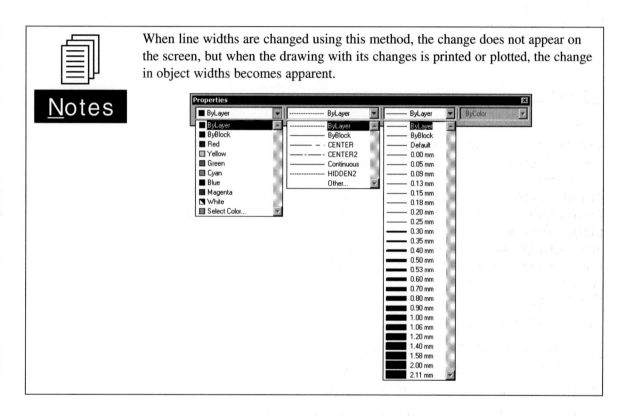

When line widths are changed using this method, the change does not appear on the screen, but when the drawing with its changes is printed or plotted, the change in object widths becomes apparent.

The UCS icon

The UCS (User Coordinate System) is of much more value when working in 3D (three-dimensions) than when working in 2D. The UCS icon is usually showing in the bottom left-hand corner of the AutoCAD window. It can be turned off by:

Command: *enter* **ucsicon** *right-click*
Enter an option [ON/OFF/All/Noorigin/ORigin/Properties] <ON>: *enter* **off** *right-click*
Command:

and the icon disappears from the screen.

When calling the command if the response to the prompts is **p (Properties)** the **UCS Icon** dialog appears. In this dialog, changes can be effected to the appearance of the icon.

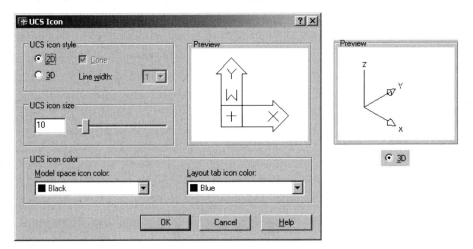

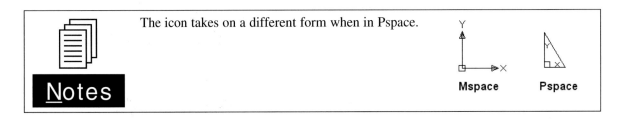

The icon takes on a different form when in Pspace.

Mspace   Pspace

Text justification

Text can be justified as to its position determined by the start point. When Single Line Text is called the command line shows:

Command: *enter* **dt** *right-click*
Specify start point of text or [Justify/Style]: *enter* **j (Justify)** *right-click*
Enter an option [Align/Fit/Center/Middle/Right/TL/TC/TR/ML/MR/BL/BC/BR]:

Some of these justifications are shown below – all from the same start point.

This is text justified to Top Left

This text justified Top Centre

This is text justified Top Right

This is text justified Middle Left

This is text justified Middle Centre

This is text justified Middle Right

This is text justified Bottom Left

This is text justified Bottom Centre

This is text justified Bottom Right

The Purge tool

If changes have been made to a drawing by erasing or modifying, it may well be that when the drawing is saved to file that it may be using more disk space than necessary because some of the objects not needed may still be in the data of the drawing. If it is thought that modifications to a drawing need to be purged of unwanted data, the **Purge** tool can be used to reduce the size of the file on disk. Not only does this make the file size smaller, but smaller drawing files load more quickly.

To call the tool *enter* **purge** or **pu** at the command line:

Command: *enter* **purge** *right-click.*

The **Purge** dialog appears. *Click* the **Purge All** button and make a selection from the **Confirm Purge** dialog which appears.

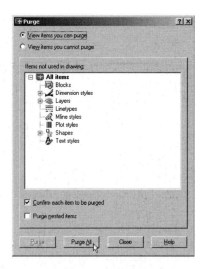

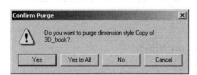

Assignments

1. Construct outlines for the hatched areas to the dimensions as shown. Then:

   (a) Hatch the outlines using the **SOLID** hatch pattern.

   (b) Set text style to **Times New Roman** set to **Bold** style and of height **10**. Add the text as shown.

2. Construct a polyline rectangle of line width **1** to the sizes as given. Then:

   (a) Judging sizes from the rectangle just drawn, construct four circles.

   (b) Hatch the area between the two outer circles using the **SOLID** hatch pattern.

   (c) Construct a closed rectangular polyline of line width **1** for the upper vertical "spoke". Array the spoke **36** times around the centre of the wheel.

   (d) Set text style top **ARIAL** set to **Bold** and of height **8** and add the text.

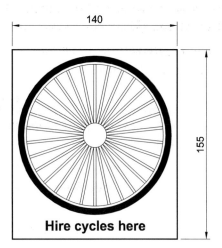

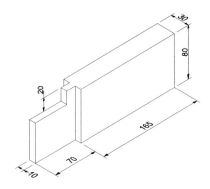

3. Construct the isometric drawing of a length of wood with a tenon cut on one end to the dimensions as shown.

4. Set a new layer **Hatch**. Then:

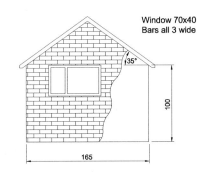

Window 70x40
Bars all 3 wide

(a) Construct the end view of a house to the given dimensions.

(b) Set the layer **Hatch** as the current layer.

(c) Using the polyline tool draw a boundary for the hatched area using the **Arc** and **Second** prompts.

(d) Hatch the area using one of the **Brick** hatch patterns.

5. Construct the title and name rectangle in any convenient part of the drawing area using the text style **Arial** set to convenient heights. Then:

(a) Construct the given view of a bolt.

(b) Set up a new layer **Construction** and make it current.

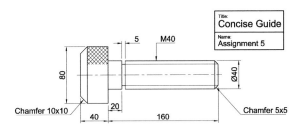

Title:
Concise Guide

Name:
Assignment 5

(c) Draw a line limiting the bottom area of the hatching.

(d) Make layer **0** current.

(e) Hatch the upper part of the bolt head.

(f) Turn layer **Hatch** off.

6. Construct a rectangle for the label and add the text **Name:** and **Number:** (top left-hand drawing). Then:

(a) Add an attributes **NAME** and **NUMBER** using a Tag **NAME**, a Prompt **Position** and a Value **Thomas**.

(b) Add a second attribute using a Tag **NUMBER**, a Prompt **Place** and a Value **01**.

(c) Save the drawing to a suitable file name.

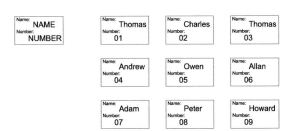

(d) Open a new drawing template and **Insert** the file nine times.

(e) Using the **Edit Attribute** tool edit each label in the drawing to produce the result shown in the right-hand drawing.

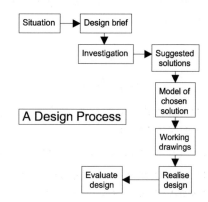

7. With text style set to **Arial** of suitable heights, construct the flow chart of **A Design Process** as shown.

8. Construct the five electronics symbols shown in the left-hand set of drawings below and save each one separately as a block. Then:

(a) Construct the electronics circuit from part of a fire alarm system given in the right-hand drawing.

(b) Add donuts (inner radius **0**, outer radius **5**) at positions as indicated.

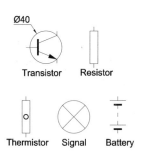

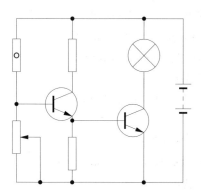

9. Construct the filleted rectangle and the small polyline shown in the left-hand drawing below. Then:

(a) Array the small rounded end polyline five times.

(b) Copy the array to the right-hand end of the rectangle.

(c) Construct the outline at the lower end of the rectangle to the dimensions as shown.

(d) Using the **Edit Polyline** tool change the lower outline to a joined polyline.

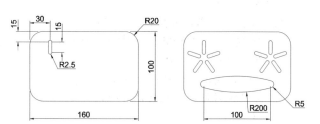

10. Call the **A3_template.dwt** template. Then:

   (a) Using the **Insert** tool insert your answers to exercises **1**, **2**, **3**, **4** and **7** into the template.

   (b) Complete the title block with suitable text using any text style.

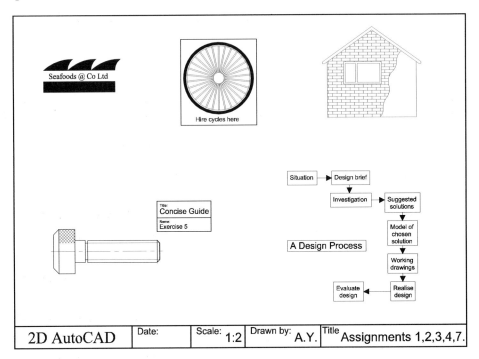

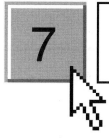

Chapter Seven

Theory of 2D Application of CAD

Here are 100 questions designed for testing what has been learned from Chapters 4, 5 and 6. In the following series of questions, the multi-part questions mostly have a single answer, but where it is thought there is more than one answer make sure all are named.

1. What is the command line abbreviation for the tool **Move**?

  (a) mov

  (b) mo

  (c) m

  (d) mm

2. What is the command line abbreviation for the tool **Mirror**?

  (a) m

  (b) mir

  (c) mi

  (d) mirr

3. What happens when the **Y** is *entered* when responding to the prompt **Delete old objects <N>:** of the **Mirror** prompts sequence?

  (a) The **Mirror** sequence stops.

  (b) The object(s) being mirrored appear as if rotated through 180°.

  (c) The object(s) being mirrored disappear from the screen.

  (d) The object{s) being mirrored appear in a different part of the screen.

4. Is a circle affected by the **Stretch** tool?

  (a) There is no reason why a circle cannot be stretched.

  (b) A circle cannot be altered by using the tool.

  (c) A circle can be stretched to form an ellipse with the aid of the tool.

  (d) A circle will be placed in another position when the tool is used.

5. In which direction would you expect a vertical line to rotate when the **Rotate** tool is used to rotate the line by 225°?

  (a) South East

  (b) South West

  (c) North West

  (d) North East

6. What are the abbreviations for the tools:

  (a) Break

  (b) Scale

  (c) Stretch

  (d) Rotate

  (e) Extend

7. How can the abbreviation **mm** be included with dimensions in a drawing?

    (a) By making a setting in a dialog box.

    (b) By *entering* **mm** after a dimension at the command line.

    (c) The abbreviation appears automatically.

8. How can the prefix **approx** be included before all dimensions in a drawing?

9. To include a horizontal dimension in a drawing, which abbreviation is *entered* at the command line and which dimension tool could be used to include the same dimension?

10. To include a vertical dimension in a drawing dimensions, which dimension tool must be selected from the **Dimensions** toolbar?

11. If the dimension **Holes Ø15** is to be included in a drawing, which dimension tool would you use and how is the word **Holes** included?

12. How can the degrees symbol be included with a **Leader** dimension?

    (a) By making settings in a dialog.

    (b) By *entering* **%%d** after a dimension at the command line.

    (c) By *entering* **degrees** after a dimension at the command line.

    (d) It is not possible.

13. How is the symbol for diameter (Ø) placed in text in AutoCAD?

14. What text must be *entered* at the command line in order for the following text to shown in the AutoCAD window:

    (a) **125±00.5**

    (b) **Ø50**

    (c) **60°**

    (d) **Ø75**

15. How are dimension styles set?

    (a) From the command line.

    (b) From the **Text Style** dialog.

    (c) From a **Dimension Style Manager** dialog.

    (d) By calling **ddim** and making settings in a dialog which appears.

16. If you set a new text style in the **Text Style** dialog, does text for the dimension style also change?

17. What is the abbreviation for a **radius** dimension when adding from the command line?

    (a) **rad**

    (b) **r**

    (c) **ra**

    (d) the full word **radius** must be *entered*.

18. When using the dimension tool **Linear Dimension**, there are two methods by which the dimension can be added to a drawing. Describe these two methods.

19. What is the abbreviation for a dimension for an **angle** dimension when adding dimensions to a drawing from the command line?

    (a) **angle**

    (b) **an**

    (c) **ang**

    (d) **a**

20. What is a geometrical tolerance dimension?

21. How is the **Dimension Style Manager** called to screen from the **Dimension** toolbar?

    (a) It is not possible to do so.

    (b) By a *left-click* in the **Dim Style Control** field.

    (c) With a *left-click* in the left-hand icon in the **Dimension** toolbar.

    (d) By closing the **Dimension** toolbar and *entering* **dimstyle** at the command line.

22. What is the purpose of the **Quick Dimension** tool in the **Dimension** toolbar?

   (a) It enables dimensions to be added o a drawing speedily.

   (b) Dimension can be added one after the other by *clicking* on parts of the drawing.

   (c) It is used to delete dimension from a drawing quickly.

   (d) It can be used to override existing dimensions quickly.

23. Why use layers when constructing drawings in AutoCAD?

   (a) Layers make for easier drawing construction.

   (b) Layers allow different drawings to be constructed and saved top the same file name.

   (c) Layers allow different line types to be used when constructing a drawing.

   (d) Layer can be turned off or on to show or hide parts of a drawing.

24. How are different line types allocated to layers?

25. Can you list the settings you have made to construct a drawing template file for your own use?

26. Why use a floppy disk for saving your templates and drawings?

   (a) To provide backup files of your drawings.

   (b) Allows files of drawings to be taken away from the computer in use.

   (c) The computer in use may be used by other operators.

   (d) Prevents any corruption of the hard disk of the computer being used at the time.

27. What is the advantage of using polylines when constructing technical drawings in AutoCAD?

28. Why turn a layer **Off**?

29. Why **Freeze** a layer?

   (a) It prevents any detail on the layer from being erased.

   (b) The layer is hidden so details cannot be added to the layer.

   (c) Only the frozen layer can be used.

   (d) All other layers are turned off.

30. Why **Lock** a layer? What is the purpose of locking a layer?

31. Would you prefer using **Construction Lines** when setting out a technical drawing?

32. How many layers can be included in a drawing constructed in AutoCAD?

33. When drawing a plan in first angle projection, which side of the front view is the plan placed?

34. If working in third angle projection where is a plan placed in respect to the position of the front view?

35. When working in orthographic projection, how many views can be included in a drawing?

   (a) 3

   (b) 2

   (c) As many as thought necessary.

   (d) It does not matter.

36. Is isometric drawing a true 3D (three-dimensional) drawing?

37. Which operations do the keys **F5**, **F7**, **F8** and **F9** toggle (turn on/off)?

38. What is an isocircle?

   (a) It is a circle in an isometric drawing.

   (b) It is an ellipse in an isometric drawing.

   (c) It is a circle formed on an isoplane.

   (d) There is no such object in an AutoCAD drawing.

39. What is the difference between a block and a wblock?

    (a) There is no difference.

    (b) Both blocks and wblocks are included in the data of a drawing file.

    (c) wblocks can be saved as separate drawings in their own right, whereas blocks are contained in the data of the drawing in which they were constructed.

    (d) Blocks can be saved as separate drawing files.

40. Have you looked at the "libraries" of symbols for building, engineering, electric and electronic drawings available in the directory **C:\Program File\AutoCAD 2002\Sample\DesignCenter**?

41. It is sometimes necessary to explode a block into is individual objects. How is this done?

42. Why is it necessary to *pick* a **base point** when constructing a block?

    (a) To ensure the drawing is placed in a correct position when it is inserted.

    (b) Because it is requested from in the **Block Definition** dialog.

    (c) Because the drawing of a block requires a starting point from which it can be constructed.

    (d) To ensure the **base point** is at the coordinate point $x,y = 0,0$.

43. An isocircle is:

    (a) a true ellipse;

    (b) a shape similar to an ellipse seen only when constructing isometric drawings;

    (c) a circle;

    (d) a distorted ellipse.

44. Three methods of calling the **Plot** tool have been described in this chapter. Can you name all three methods?

45. How does one change from **Mspace** to **Pspace**?

46. When in **Paper Space** What is the name given to the dialog from which print/plot parameters are set?

    (a) Plot

    (b) Print

    (c) Page Setup – Layout1

    (d) Print/Plot Setup.

47. What is the purpose of the **Window>** button in the **Plot** dialog.

    (a) A *left-click* on the button closes the dialog and brings back the AutoCAD window.

    (b) To bring up the window showing the appearance of the plotted drawing.

    (c) To window the drawing on screen to preview the plot.

    (d) To show a full preview of the plot.

48. What is the difference between the results of a *left-click* on the **Full Preview** and a *left-click* on the **Partial Preview** button?

49. Set variables have been referred to on several occasions in the pages of this book. What are set variables?

    (a) Set methods of setting up a variety of drawing templates.

    (b) Set methods by which drawing tools and editing tools are used.

    (c) A variety of methods by which the size of the drawing screen is determined.

    (d) The sizes of dialogs as they appear on screen.

50. Grips are of use for which purpose?

(a) For holding an object in a drawing in its correct position.

(b) For quickly using some editing tools on an object.

(c) To switch over to editing tools when using a **Draw** tool.

(d) To show osnap positions on an object in a drawing.

51. A DXF file can be used for saving a drawing to file when:

(a) the drawing is to be opened in another CAD software system;

(b) a drawing cannot be saved as a file with the AutoCAD extension *.dxf;

(c) a drawing is to be saved for inserting into another drawing;

(d) the drawing contains blocks or xrefs.

52. What are raster files?

53. What is the value of using the **Properties** window?

(a) It shows the size of the file to which a drawing can be saved.

(b) It allows editing of any part of a drawing on screen.

(c) Drawings can be *dragged* from the window into a drawing on screen.

(d) It lists all the drawings which have earlier been saved to disk.

54. How is the **Properties** window brought to screen?

55. What is an attribute?

56. Which of these statements is/are correct?

(a) Modifications and corrections can always be added to a drawing in Paper Space.

(b) Modifications and corrections can only be added to a drawing in Paper Space if the **Model – Paper Space** button is set to **MODEL**.

(c) Modifications and corrections can only be added to a drawing in Paper Space if the **Model – Paper Space** button is set to **PAPER**.

(d) Modifications and corrections can never be made to a drawing in Paper Space.

57. Which of these statements is/are correct?

(a) The set variable **TILEMODE** should always be set to **1**.

(b) The set variable **TILEMODE** should always be set to **0**.

(c) When the set variable **TILEMODE** is set to **0** the drawing on screen will be in Paper Space.

(d) When the set variable **TILEMODE** is set to **1** the drawing on screen will be in Paper Space.

58. How are drawings placed in the **Multiple Design Environment**?

59. Which of these statements is/are correct?

(a) Only four drawings can be placed in the **MDE** at any one time.

(b) Only two drawings can be placed in the **MDE** at any one time.

(c) There is no limit to the number of drawings which can be opened in the **MDE**.

(d) The limit to the number of drawings that can be opened in the **MDE** is confined to the amount of memory available in the computer in use.

60. Can drawings be constructed in **Paper Space**?

  (a) No – it is not possible. Drawings can only be constucted in **Model Space**.

  (b) Yes – drawings can be constructed in **Paper Space**, but only when a paper space drawing template is opened.

  (c) Yes – drawings can be constructed in **Paper Space** without opening a template.

  (d) Yes – providing the **MODEL** button is set **on**.

61. The abbreviation for the **Distance** tool when called from the command line is?

  (a) dis

  (b) dist

  (c) di

  (d) d

62. The **Divide** tool is used for showing division points along an object in a drawing. How are the division points displayed?

  (a) They show automatically as short vertical lines.

  (b) They show automatically as short sloping lines.

  (c) A point must first be set from the **Point Style** dialog.

  (d) Dots from at the division points.

63. List the properties which can be changed in any part of a drawing with the use of the **Properties** palette (AutoCAD 2004) or window (previous AutoCAD's).

64. Dimensions can be placed in drawings by calling the dimension tools from the command line. The abbreviation for calling dimensions in this manner is:

  (a) ddim

  (b) di

  (c) dim

  (d) d.

65. How can a layer be frozen?

66. When a layer is frozen:

  (a) details on the frozen layer cannot be seen on screen;

  (b) nothing can be added to the frozen layer;

  (c) objects on screen cannot be modified;

  (d) freezing a layer is the same as turning a layer off.

67. Construction lines are of infinite length. Can you explain why this is so?

68. In first angle orthographic projection the plan is placed:

  (a) below a front view;

  (b) below an end view;

  (c) to the right of a front view;

  (d) above a front view.

69. In third angle orthographic projection:

  (a) an end view is placed on the opposite side of a front view to the direction in which the view is seen;

  (b) on the same side as the direction from which the end view is viewed;

  (c) below the front view;

  (d) above the front view.

70. What is an isoplane?

71. Isoplanes can be set by pressing the key:

  (a) F2;

  (b) F6;

  (c) F4;

  (d) F5.

72. What is the difference between a block and a wblock?

73. When placing a block in a drawing it must be:

    (a) exploded;

    (b) it can be placed in an exploded state;

    (c) it can be or need not be exploded;

    (d) it never is exploded.

73. What is the difference between a block inserted into a drawing and one inserted using the **xref** tool?

74. In AutoCAD 2004 the **DesignCenter** is a palette. What is the difference between a palette and a Windows window?

75. Drawings can be placed from the **DesignCenter** by:

    (a) copying from the DesignCenter;

    (b) *dragging* from the DesignCenter;

    (c) by closing the DesignCenter and opening from a dialog;

    (d) drawings cannot be placed in AutoCAD from the DesignCenter.

76. What is the abbreviation for the **Purge** tool:

    (a) **pur**;

    (b) **p**;

    (c) **pu**;

    (d) **pp**.

77. From which toolbar can the **Move** tool be called:

    (a) from the **Draw** toolbar;

    (b) from the **Modify** toolbar;

    (c) from the **Standard** toolbar;

    (d) it cannot be called from a toolbar.

78. When using the **Stretch** tool:

    (a) circles can be stretched;

    (b) circles can only be affected by the tool if they are part of a drawing;

    (c) circles are unaffected by the tool;

    (d) instead of being stretched, circles are moved by the tool.

79. When using the **Rotate** tool, rotation takes place in:

    (a) an anticlockwise direction;

    (b) a clockwise direction;

    (c) a clockwise direction;

    (d) in any direction.

80. The **Distance** tool is used for:

    (a) marking distances along lines;

    (b) placing points between measured distances;

    (c) as a ruler;

    (d) for measuring distances between selected points.

81. What is the use of the **Area** tool?

82. From which toolbar can the **Area** tool be called?

    (a) From the **Draw** toolbar.

    (b) From the **Inquiry** toolbar.

    (c) From the **Modify** toolbar.

    (d) The tool can only be called by *entering* area at the command line.

83. What are **Grips** and what are they used for?

84. **Grips** can be disabled:

   (a) by calling the **Grips** dialog and disabling the **Grips** radio button;

   (b) by *entering* a set variable and responding with a **0**;

   (c) they cannot be disabled and are always functioning when required;

85. DXF files can be opened in most CAD software applications.

   (a) This is not true.

   (b) DXF files can only be opened in CAD software published by Autodesk.

   (c) Yes – DXF files can be opened in most CAD software systems.

   (d) DXF files can only be opened in AutoCAD.

86. The **Properties** window or palette can be opened by pressing the following keys:

   (a) **Ctrl+T**

   (b) **Ctrl+1**

   (c) **F2**

   (d) **Shift+3**

87. Is it necessary to set the linetype scale when setting up a template?

88. A drawing includes a block which has attributes. What is an attribute?

   (a) It is an object in the block which can be changed.

   (b) It is a note attached to the block which can be modified.

   (c) It can be used to delete the block from the drawing.

   (d) It is a set of dimensions for the block which can be edited.

89. A transparent command is:

   (a) one which can be used when other commands are active;

   (b) one which can only be used when a block is inserted into a drawing;

   (c) one which can be used in place of other commands;

   (d) one which repeats a previously used command.

90. When using certain tools from the **Modify** toolbar on dimensioned drawings, the dimensions are said to be associative. What is meant by associative in this sense?

   (a) If the dimensions are copied they can be used on another part of the drawing.

   (b) The dimensions change as the tool is used to accommodate to the new modification.

   (c) The dimensions must be redrawn.

   (d) The dimensions are no longer attached to the part which has been modified.

91. If it is necessary to take part of a drawing from the layer **0 to** layer text, which tool would be used?

   (a) **Move**

   (b) **Mirror**

   (c) **Copy**

   (d) **Change**

92. The width of any object in a drawing can changed. There are two ways in which such a change can be carried out. What are these two methods?

93. When constructing an electronic circuit which includes a number of different symbols, the best way of constructing the symbols for the circuit would be to:

(a) carefully construct each and every symbol in its correct position in the circuit.

(b) construct each symbol separately and save it as a wblock;

(c) construct each symbol separately and save it as a block;

(d) *drag* symbols from the DesignCenter into the AutoCAD darwing area.

94. What is the purpose of a set variable? Explain this with reference to the set variable **pellipse**.

95. When a drawing is constructed in AutoCAD and saved to file, automatically a backup drawing is saved. In the file system what is the drawing extension name of this backup file?

(a) *.dwt

(b) *.dw

(c) *.bak

(d) *bakup

96. How would it be possible to change a backup file into a usable drawing file?

97. A drawing has been constructed in Mspace. In order to plot the drawing it has been decided to place the drawing in Pspace. How can any necessary changes be made to the drawing when it is in Pspace?

(a) The changes can be made without any further actions.

(b) The **MODEL** button in the status bar must first be *clicked* to change it to **PAPER**.

(c) It is necessary to go back into Mspace before changes can be made.

(d) Once in Pspace it is not possible to make changes.

98. When changing from Mspace to Pspace, a viewport border is seen surrounding the drawing in Pspace. This border can be hidden. Outline the steps necessary to hide the viewport border.

99. If a number of modifications have been made to a drawing, when it is saved to file, there may be unnecessary data in the file, which can be removed before the drawing is saved. How can this be achieved?

(a) By using the **Erase** tool.

(b) By saving the file using the **Save As** command rather than the **Save** command.

(c) By using the **Purge** tool.

(d) By being careful not to include any unwanted objects in the drawing.

100. If a drawing file is to be renamed, what is the easiest method of so doing?

101. An isometric drawing is:

(a) a 2D drawing;

(b) a 3D drawing;

(c) an accurate 3D drawing;

(d) a representation of a 3D drawing.

Index